Bowls Cookbook

100 healthful one-dish meals, satisfying and nutritious combos to fuel and bless your day + 12 New Recipes

By

Emma Watson

Table of Contents

"Bowl meals" is a popular fad that's here to remain. Sure, there'll be occasions once we need our meals served in classes, but from the daily search to eat delectable food that actually disturbs you the bowl is the go-to.

Most of us wish for a fantastic bowl. But what creates a bowl which is more than only a random pile of leftovers? Well, I have spent the past couple of years producing bowls and composed a book on it, known as great bowls of food, I have some ideas and shortcuts for producing dinner or lunch at a bowl.

Engage your senses

Look: the initial impression of how a bowl comes via your eyes. A fantastic bowl is pinterest-worthy, using a lively mixture of vibrant foods composed on top. Shade is essential.

Smell: consider your sense of smell, also, and lure that the diner with attractive scents, such as ginger and curry, garlic and other spices.

Taste: obviously, an excellent bowl needs to have sufficient tastes going to maintain your mouth amused with each bite. It is essential to the entire bowl encounter you own an assortment of "taste zones," so you are able to take a snack of something sour, and then something salty, then some thing a bit more creamy.

Chew: using a nicely written bowl, you've got a lot of great shades, and a good deal of chewy and crispy sensations in precisely the exact same mouthful.

Construct your bowl

Bowls all begin with a foundation. Distribute the bottom of your own bowl with something comparatively impartial, such as whole grains, legumes, legumes, zucchini or celery, or perhaps beans or legumes for a protein intake. You will see that all those foods are high in fiber and nutrition, including white plain or rice noodles. Whole grains have more feel, also, and their plump, occasionally crunchy texture increases the experience.

A number of the top bowls begin with quinoa, brown rice oats, however, do not be reluctant to try out wheat, buckwheat or wheat berries, even for much more whole grain pleasure. Bonus points onto this region of the bowl include once you scatter a little sauce or dressing on the foundation and blend it before putting the other components in addition to

In addition to your foundation, you will need colour, pinch and an variety of tastes. That is obviously best achieved with large amounts of vegetables. A few of slivered kale one side is a lush comparison to a pile of shredded carrots, shining with crimson goodness. Scarlet pickled beets, red peppers or berries provide you a few red to make all of it pop. Be certain that you season every veggie since it moves, even if it's only having a pinch of salt or spoonful of tamari or warm sauce.

Your proteins may be thrilling, also, as you choose the perfect match to all that's happening under. Toss some rotten meat in skillet? Roast lettuce in teriyaki? Or only rinse some canned legumes and provide them a dab of vinegar. Nuts and seeds up the protein, also, and include good crunch. A couple of cashews or walnuts are able to effect a drab bowl unexpectedly irresistible.

Now come the last bits, the toppings which produce or break a excellent bowl. Is the sauce or dressing will be drizzled tantalizingly within the piles and heaps of colorful vegetables? Make certain that it's a flavor-packed one, also do not be timid with extreme flavors like ginger, garlic, green cheeses, spices, miso and very good oils. Balance sour and sweet, enjoying soy, honey and rice vinegar collectively, or skillet sauce with a dollop or two of dijon mustard along with wake up your palate. Give the entire occasion a jolt with a pinch of kimchi or even pickles of any sort, a loaf of bread, or any surprising sweet bits.

As soon as you attempt some fantastic bowl recipes, then you will find the hang it, and also learn how to customize dishes for all of your moods, in addition to your loved ones members and friends.

How to create a much better bowl

Gorgeous nourish bowls really are really far greater than the usual salad. Also called buddha bowls or prosperity bowls, these hot meals supply you with a bounty of plant foods in 1 dish. This sexy menu thing is a fantastic healthier option when exercising, but what is even better, is the fact that nourish bowls are fast and simple to create at home also.

There is no demand for a recipe -- that is the best dish to use up leftovers and whatever vegetables you have on your refrigerator -- you simply have to construct a fantastic balance of protein, carbs, greensalong with other veggies and wholesome fats.

Listed below are the 6 easy actions to creating the great nourish jar:

- Measure 1 -- begin with a foundation of fantastic quality carbs. Ideally search for wholegrain choices like wild or brown rice, quinoa or soba noodles, even since these are inclined to be low gi and provide you energy.
- Measure two -- shirt your foundation with two --3 cups of lettuce greens for heaps of nutrient abundant goodness. Believe lettuce, rocket, lettuce and mixed leaves and also do not overlook these zingy fresh herbs such as coriander and mint.
- Measure 3 -- proceed to the construct with half of a cup of protein. If you're constructing a more meat-free bowl, perfect protein choices have been broccoli, tempeh, beans, legumes, and legumes.
- Measure 4 -- longer veggies! This time it is not the leafy greens however vegetables such as pumpkin, capsicum, carrots, edamame, tomatoes, and pineapple. Add half a cup of your favorites. They could go in uncooked for extra pinch or roasted and caramelised such as large, bold flavours or even a mix of both. Aim to blend the colors for more nourishment.
- Measure 5 -- do not overlook some healthful fats to make the dish together and also enhance the flavours. It is difficult to go beyond a few creamy avocado along with the pinch of seeds and nuts.
- Measure 6 -- it off with a few ribbons of dressing. This is sometimes as straightforward as extra virgin coconut oil and a squeeze of lemon or to get a larger punch pick one of many choices of yummy asian bites.

As soon as you've got the fundamentals, it is possible to power your bowl match with a few wise nourishment pairings. Some meals function better in pairs assisting your system unlock and much more readily access minerals and vitamins.

Listed below are a couple tasty mixes to test:

- If you couple sweet potato (a source of vitamin c) with lettuce (a supply of iron) it helps enhance your iron intake.
- Pairing a healthful fat with a few veggies helps along with your vitamin intake. Carrots include vitamin a, while vitamin is full of vitamins k and e. These vitamins are fat thus when consumed with great fats such as those in nuts, peanuts and seeds, so it's easier for your body to absorb these minerals.

- Mushrooms, broccoli along with haloumi produce excellent bowl components and in addition, they bring out the greatest supplements in every other. Mushrooms are full of vitamin d while kale and haloumi are full of calcium, both of which assist build strong bones and wholesome teeth.

The last tip for constructing a bowl that is better is to keep each of the various ingredients different, as opposed to mixing them all together. Though your bowl does not have to be instagram fine, we really do consume our own eyes and study indicates that eating yummy looking food will make you feeling more fulfilled.

Best 10 health benefits of bowling

Bowling also supplies you with numerous health advantages.

1. Muscle strengthening and toning: bowling helps encourage muscle exercise of their body, as you're doing a great deal of walking together with the excess burden of a bowling ball into your palms. Further, once you're extending your arm to throw the bowling ball, then the extending and bending that happens provides sufficient exercise for those tendons, ligaments, tendons, joints and muscles in arms.

2. Weight reduction: bowling helps slim down by speeding up your metabolism. Even though the match is confined to a tiny region, your continuous motion whilst playing helps burn off extra fat. You are working out your legs while walking back and forth, and running the remainder of your body as you lift and fold the bowling ball down the lane. The normal bowler walks roughly 3/5ths of a mile through a three-game chain.

3. Boost social life: around two million bowlers bowl and socialize together each week at leagues during america, as stated by the bowling foundation. Bowling teams and leagues permit you to meet fellow gamers and spend some time with old buddies. Locating companionship via bowling teams and leagues may facilitate loneliness from the elderly and many others who live independently, reducing strain and depression. Social connections around shared interests can boost longevity.

4. Reduce threat of disorder: a sedentary lifestyle is among the primary risk factors for cardiovascular disease, according to webmd. Exercise, such as bowling, reduces your chance of stroke, heart ailments, diabetes, increases bone density, and improves blood circulation, reduces cholesterol levels and blood pressure, and aids your body use oxygen. Attempt to bowl or twice every week for optimal benefits.

5. Could be enjoyed at any point: bowling is one of those few sports which lets you compete at any given point and become an expert. The sport is appreciated by everyone from preschoolers to senior citizens and is now the fastest growing school varsity game. There is a minimal risk of harm, making it a favorite game for elderly folks. Many bowling alleys can adapt people in wheelchairs along with bowlers that are blind.

6. Anxiety assist: from engaging in physical action, bowling makes it possible for us to alleviate daily anxiety. Socializing with people throughout the game also functions as a psychological stress reliever.

7. Simple to find out: it promotes simple adjustment procedures, and that's the reason why it's enjoyed by the majority of kids and grownups. In the view of 95 percent bowlers, it could be played for recreation, comfort, competitively and socially. The ease of the game is now making it a favourite game of people all around the world.

8. Healthy heart: relationships and relationships constructed in this game assists in better functionality of muscles. Additionally, the adrenaline that's sensed during a game also raises heart rate. Bowling hence promotes a healthy heart.

9. Interesting for the entire household: a big contributing factor to this simplicity of the game is that the immense adaptability it provides. The principles of the sport are extremely simple to comprehend and understand, along with also the automatic scoring approaches take care of all of the scoring to you. Participants love this game because they enjoy the competition that accompanies it but due to the pleasure they have and also the simplicity by which they can pass time with their loved ones members and friends.

10. Hand-eye coordination: mixing the hockey ball and hitting pins needs a wonderful deal of hand-eye manipulation. This type of focus stimulates mental alertness, concentration and strategic strategy. This makes the ideal match for young folks to hone motor abilities and hand-eye coordination, also for elderly individuals to refine strategies.

7 steps to creating a healthy dinner bowl with no recipe

The idea is straightforward: you require a bowlput whole foods in it, mix and dress itand consume it. A dinner bowl isn't hard to throw together on any given weeknight after work, making it a fantastic choice to anything else you were going to pop into the microwave. It is even simpler if you've got a stash of precooked grains to mass up your mealit prevents you from needing to take some opportunity to create a pot of rice or farro immediately.

The options and possibilities are infinite, which is either freeing or overpowering. Should you truly need recipes, then sara forte includes an entire cookbook devoted to dishes, called appropriately, " the sprouted kitchen bowl and spoon. Do not be reluctant to experiment in your own here, since it is a really forgiving arrangement.

There is a fundamental arrangement into a bowl, so you can learn how to make it with no recipe. The human anatomy is or some combination of these: carbohydrates, legumes, lentils, greens, lettuce, lettuce, plus sauce. Here, we will discuss how to construct your dinner dish, which will provide you the assurance to break with snacks and toss a tasty, satisfying dinner every night of the week.

1. Grains

Grains, particularly when coupled with protein, also can keep you feeling satisfied for quite a while. Even though a salad may make you feeling peckish after a hour or soa bowl has been constructed around the notion that you don't wish to consume three dishes. Although you're able to create the bowl with rice or white rice since the grain, whole grains would be best. Not only are they healthier, but they still stand up better compared to the other components you will increase your meal.

To get a dinner bowlbrown rice is a good staple. Quinoa is another fantastic alternative. To get slightly more chewiness, make a kettle of farro or barley. If you are creating a skillet go for complete oats. You wish to target for well-cooked sausage which are not either undercooked or completely mushy, since they take a fantastic size part of everything you are eating. For hints on creating the ideal batch of brown riceread this post from eating well. Among the best suggestions is to let it break until you dig, which makes it possible for the starches from the grain to business a little and averts mushiness.

2. Protein

Especially, well-seasoned protein. This may be plant or animal protein, based upon your diet tastes (or anything is on your fridge). Simply cook it, then slice it upand then add a few to a bowl.

For an asian-inspired bowl, then grill some miso-ginger marinated salmon in bobby flay. As an alternative, you can consume this crispy peanut kale out of minimalist baker and serve over brown rice. A bowl can readily be accomplished with this walnut balsamic-glazed tempeh out of meghan telpner or that greek noodle poultry in budget bytes. Both are good with farro.

A flank steak may be flipped to guy fieri's broiled tequila garlic carrot beef to get a bowl that is mexican, along with chipotle-lime broiled pork loin from alton brown will taste good on brown rice or quinoa.

3. Legumes

For an excess piece of protein and fiber, or as a fast option to a substantial protein, then add some beans to a bowl. Just like the protein in the former page, be sure they are well-seasoned. In fact, everything on your bowl ought to be well-seasoned.

Lentils are excellent at a tropical or indo-asian bowl, in addition to in any sort of farmer's marketplace bowl. Green lentils have a tendency to be better suited to a bowlas they don't secure stewy like red peas do. If you are unfamiliar with cooking peas or want a few hints, the kitchn includes a fantastic article on the topic. Stewed black beans such as these out of chowhound really are a wonderful addition to some mexican-type bowl, even whilst pinto beans would be the go-to to get a skillet.

4. Greens

Dark, leafy greens include a pop of colour against the beiges of proteins and grains, but in addition they add important minerals and vitamins. If you are a lover of spinach, it's possible to simply finely chopped or shred a few lacinato (also referred to as dino or tuscan) lettuce and then put it directly into a bowl. Some bowls are far much better suited to some fast cooked green. If you are creating a brown rice and also miso-ginger salmon bowl, then catch a few baby bok choi and immediately sauté it, then halved.

Sautéed spinach or chard is always a fantastic idea, as can be a number of arugula. Beet greens and watercress are equally great for farmer's market-type bowls. Broccoli raab may be an excellent addition to your bowl, however, you absolutely wish to cook it to decrease its own bitterness. To get a listing of hot greens and comprehension concerning the way to prepare every, mention this post from epicurious.

5. Vegetables

Between the greens as well as the veggies, forte attempts to create her dishes least half vegetables. It retains the meal not allowing the the protein escape control. This might be shaved carrot ribbons, roasted brussels sprouts, or thin-skinned delicata skillet roasted at high heat such as this recipe from eatingwell.

It might be fresh diced bell peppers or even sautéed chopped bell peppers, or it might be bits of grilled zucchini and eggplant. It might be steamed noodle or crunchy, roasted broccoli florets. It might be chopped cherry tomatoes or cucumbers or red raw or cabbage, foul-smelling candy corn wrapped off the cob. When there's a vegetable from the aisle, you have these options: dish it, roast it, either sauté this, or make it raw. Do not feel as though you want to adhere to only one, possibly; blend and match for an enjoyable and intriguing bowl.

6. Toppings

Add a little additional texture and taste to a bowl using a sprinkling of toppings. This might be a couple of roasted seeds or nuts or chopped veggies. It might be crumbled goat milk to get tanginess or feta to get just a tiny saltiness. It might be a couple of pieces of perfectly ripe avocado or even any fruit which matches the tastes already within the dish, such as chopped tomatoes with balsamic vinegar. It might be a loaf of crunchy peppers or toasted oats. It might be breadcrumbs or even croutons, also. Only a little something to generate the bowl soda with a little additional pizzazz.

7. Dressing or sauce

There should always be a great sauce. That is what twists all of the parts of the jar together. Give it a fantastic drizzle along with a strong throw, and you are all set. Some sauce suggestions to get you started:

- Attempt a nutty tahini sauce similar to that one from dishing up the dirt.
- Create a spoonful cashew sauce to get a just sweet, refreshing, and creamy raise into a bowl with this particular recipe in pinch of yum.
- To bring along a mexican-inspired dish, mix this up sweet, smoky, somewhat spicy chipotle sauce out of the garden grazer.
- This sweet and sour honey skillet in the kitchn will liven up some poultry jar.
- A flexible dressing table, this thai peanut sauce out of coffee and quinoa may be utilized as a salad dressing, dipping sauce, or even to groom your own bowl.
- For a hot north african twist, create a harissa sauce such as this 1 in epicurious.

- Borrow this lemon-pesto dressing table from food network to pour any blossom bowl.

How to construct a protein bowl you may enjoy

Protein foods -- so sexy at the moment! And it is not just since they look fantastic on instagram. They're also able to meet your nutritional requirements while diluting your culinary imagination. Additionally, they are ideal meal every time of day, such as breakfast, since there are many ways to twist it.

For men and women that are too overwhelmed or busy to prepare an elaborate meal (therefore, pretty much all people!), all you will need to do is follow this simple blueprint to create a protein bowl you are guaranteed to enjoy.

Begin with the fundamentals

The components for a totally balanced protein jar may be divided into five groups: whole grains, high quality fats and healthy fats, leafy veggies and fruit. Contain a minumum of one thing from each class, and you are golden.

But that does not mean you need to play with these rules each moment. If you are not feeling such as fruit in dinner, then bypass it. Had enough protein to your day? Forget it. Just sub a component from a different class.

Subsequently get gourmet

While choosing your components, prevent things from becoming dull by contemplating different preparations: boiled, braised, pickledraw, raw, roasted, sauteed, cooked or smoked -- just to mention a couple!

Also think of the way the textures will socialize. If your bowl is seeming like it needs additional feel, finish it off with just a bit of pinch with the addition of seeds, nuts, apples or broccoli.

Finally, you do not need every snack to feel like a punch in the mouth, therefore adhere to a 3:2 ratio in regards to taste. Satisfy three deliciously flavorful components using just two less yummy ones. Finish it off with a dressing of your choice plus a two or 2.

Today b.y.o.b (construct your own bowl)

15

As soon as you've pinpointed the notion, you are prepared to get creative. Still require a little more advice? Following is a no-fail manual of go-to components to select from.

Whole grains

- Amaranth
- Barley
- Bulgur
- Brown rice
- Buckwheat
- Corn
- Faro
- Freekeh
- Kamut
- Quinoa
- Millet
- Oats
- Spelt
- Teff
- Wheat berry
- Complete rye
- Entire wheat

High-quality proteins

- Beans and legumes: adzuki beans, black beans, cowpeas, garbanzos, great northern beans, lima beans, kidney beans, pinto beans, mung beans, soybeans, split peas
- Dairy: cottage cheese, fat-free yogurt, skillet cheese, kefir
- Fish: canned salmon, mackerel
- Spicy: pork loin, pork tenderloin, center loin
- Poultry: chicken (skinless), legumes, poultry (skinless)
- Steak: bottom round, eye round roast, sirloin tip side beef, best round, top sirloin beef

Healthy fats

- Dairy: cottage cheese, kefir
- Avocados

- Nuts and legumes: almonds, brazil nuts, cashews, chia seeds, flaxseed, hazelnuts, peanuts, pumpkin seeds, sesame seeds, sunflower seeds, walnuts
- Noodle: anchovies, black cod, char, halibut, mackerel, mussels, oysters, salmon, mackerel, tuna

Nutrient-rich berries

- Beets
- Beet greens
- Broccoli
- Brussels sprouts
- Carrots
- Celery
- Collard greens
- Dandelion greens
- Kale
- Red leaf lettuce
- Seaweed
- Spinach
- Swiss chard
- Watercress

Fresh fruits

- Apples
- Banana
- Cherries
- Blueberries
- Blackberries
- Grapes
- Mango
- Peaches
- Pineapple
- Pomegranates
- Raspberries
- Strawberries
- Tomatoes

Dressings

- Balsamic vinegar
- Fish sauce
- Flaxseed oil
- Grapeseed oil
- Jojoba oil
- Spicy sauce
- Lemon juice
- Lime juice
- Coconut oil
- Pesto
- Red wine vingear
- Sesame petroleum
- Noodle sauce
- Sriracha
- Vinaigrette

Garnishes

- Chives
- Chia seeds
- Dried goji berries
- Flaxseed
- Steak
- Ginger
- Kimchi
- Pickled vegetables (carrots, cucumbers, radishes, peppers -- you name it)
- Pomegranate seeds
- Roasted red peppers
- Sesame seeds
- Sun-dried berries

1. Uncomplicated seed & grain loaf

Bake a sterile grain and seed loaf at half an hour, ideal with soup

Ingredients

1. 500g mixed grain bread

2. 1 tablespoon every sesame and poppy seeds, and additional for topping

3. 1 sachet fast-action yeast

4. 1 teaspoon salt

5. 300ml hand-hot water

6. 2 tablespoons olive oil

7. 1 tablespoon honey
Strategy

1. Tip the flourseeds, yeast and salt into a big bowl. Mix the oil and honey into a jug, then pour into the dry mixture, stirring all of the opportunity to produce a soft dough. If it feels tacky, sprinkle in a bit more flour.

2. Turn out the dough on a lightly floured surface and knead for 5 minsuntil the dough no longer feels tacky, drizzle with a bit more flour as you require it.

3. Oil a 1.2-litre loaf and set the dough in the tin, then pressing it evenly. Cover with a tea towel and leave to rise for 1 hr, till it pops back once you press it with your finger. Heat oven to 200c/fan 180c/gas 6.

4. Make eight slashes throughout the surface of the loaf, brush with warm water and scatter alternately with poppy and sesame seeds. Bake for 30-35 mins before the loaf is brown and rose. Hint it out on a cooling rack and leave to cool.

2. Timeless kedgeree

Smoky haddock, soft-boiled eggs along with also the hot spice of coriander and garlic make an extremely special brunch or dinner dish.

Ingredients

3 tablespoons vegetable oil

1 big onion, finely chopped

1 teaspoon ground coriander

1 teaspoon garlic

2 teaspoon curry powder

200g rice, rinsed under cold water

6 eggs

400ml milk

300g un-dyed smoked haddock

2 bay leaves

Little handful coriander and chopped, chopped

Strategy

1. Heat the oil and cook the onion into a bowl using a well-fitting lid till soft but not colored. Add the spices along with a few salt and then continue to cook till golden and aromatic, about 4 mins. Sprinkle on the rice and stir fry it well so all the grains are well coated. Stir in 400ml water, then raise the heat, cover the pan, then bring to the boil. After boiling, turn into a simmer and cook for 10 mins. Turn off the heat and leave to steam, covered, for 20 mins. The rice needs to be cooked in case you do not lift the lid prior to the conclusion of the moment.
2. Put eggs in a bowl and cover with warm water, then place to a high heat and bring to the boil. Simmer for 3 mins for tender, or 5-6 mins for hard-boiled. Plunge into cold water until cool enough to peel off, then triple.
3. Meanwhile, pour the milk on the haddock into a skillet and bring to a gentle simmer. Poach for 5-8 mins until cooked through and flesh flakes easily. Eliminate from the peel and discard skin and flake fish.
4. Gradually stir eggs, fish and seasoning to the rice, top with all the eggs and function.

3. Three-grain porridge

This nutritious breakfast, also made of toasted oatmeal, spelt and barley, is very easy to make and may be stored for up to six weeks

Ingredients

- 300g oatmeal
- 300g spelt flakes
- 300g wheat batter
- Agave nectar and chopped strawberries, to serve (optional)

Strategy

1. Working in batches, then pinch the oatmeal, peppermint flakes and barley at a big, dry skillet for 5 mins till golden, then leave to cool and store in an airtight container.
2. If you would like to consume that, just blend 50g of this porridge mix in a saucepan together with 300ml water or milk. Cook for 5 mins, stirring occasionally, then top with a spoonful of honey and tomatoes, if you prefer (optional). Will keep for 2 weeks.

4. Brown loaf

Try out this easy step by step brown bread recipe to create a seeded loaf or attempt one of three stunning variations.

Ingredients

1. 400g malted grain brown bread wheat, or wholemeal or granary bread flour

2. 100g powerful white bread flour

3. 7g sachet easy-bake dried yeast (or 2 teaspoon quick dried yeast)

4. 11/2 tsp salt

5. 1 tablespoon soft butter

6. 4 tablespoons mixed seed (optional), like jojoba, pumpkin, sesame and sunflower, and extra for sprinkling

Strategy

1. Mix the selection of brown bread together with all the white, the salt and yeast in a large mixing bowl. Place into the butter and rub it in the flour. Stir in the seeds when using. Create a dip at the middle of the flour and put into virtually 300ml hand heat (cool as opposed to warm) water, using a round-bladed knife.) then mix in enough of the water and also a little more if desired, to collect any dry pieces in the base of the bowl and then till the mix comes together to get a tender, not too sticky, dough. Gather it into a ball with your handson.

2. Set the dough to a very lightly floured surface and knead for 8-10 mins till it feels smooth and elastic, just including the minimum of additional flour if needed to avoid the saliva sticking. Put the ball of dough onto a lightly floured surface. Cover having the upturned, clean, big glass jar and leave 45 mins-1 hr or till doubled in size and seems springy and light. Timing will be based on the heat of this space.

3. Knock back the dough by gently kneading just 3-4 occasions. You merely wish to knock out any large air bubbles, but therefore an excessive amount of managing now will shed the dough's lightness. Shape into a ball. Cover the glass jar and leave for 15 mins.

4. Now contour to create a tin loaf grease a 1.2-litre capability loaf tin (approximately 23 x 13 x 5.5cm) and line the base with baking parchment. Together with your knuckles, flatten the dough to a rectangle roughly 25 x 19cm. Twist both shorter endings to the middle such as an envelope, then create a 1/4 twist, then sew to precisely the exact same dimensions and roll up really closely, beginning from among the ends. Roll the cover of the dough into additional seeds and set in the tin using the combine under, pressing on the seeds lightly into the soup. Cover with a clean tea towel. Leave 40-45 mins, or till climbed about 5cm above the surface of the tin.

5. Place a roasting tin at the base of the oven 20 mins before prepared to inhale and heat oven to 230c/210c fan/gas 8. Place the increased bread from the toaster, carefully pour around 250ml cold water in the roasting tin (this can hiss and make a burst of steam to provide you a crispy crust)then reduce the heat to 220c/200c fan/gas 7. Bake for approximately 30 mins or until golden, covering with foil for the past five mins if beginning to brown too fast. Leave in the tin for 2-3 mins, and then remove and cool on a wire rack. Should you tap the beneath of this baked loaf if need to be solid and firm hollow.

5. Malted pine seed loaf

Leading up to essential fatty acids, iron and calcium with this healthful and tasty bread.

Ingredients

1. 500g strong wholemeal flour (we utilized doves farm blended grain malthouse bread flour)

2. 7g sachet fast-action dried yeast

3. 1 teaspoon salt

4. Up to 350ml warm water

5. 100g mixed seed (we employed a mixture of linseeds(seeds seeds, pumpkin seeds and sesame seeds)

6. 50g walnut bits

7. Just a tiny eucalyptus oil, for instance

Strategy

- Create the dough with the flour, yeast, water and salt as mentioned in the'works nicely with' recipe (see right), including the majority of the seeds along with the peppers because you knead the dough. Leave to rise into a fresh bowl stated, then knock back and then form to a sizable circular. Roll the around at the rest of the seeds, then raise the bread on a menu to establish for around 30 mins until doubled in size.
- Heat oven to 220c/fan 200c/gas 7. Bake the bread for 15 minsthen lower the heat to 190c/fan 170c/gas 5 and then continue to bake for 30 mins before the loaf sounds hollow when tapped on the foundation. Leave the bread onto a cooling rack to cool thoroughly. The loaf will remain fresh in an airtight container for 3 days or can be frozen for 1 month.

6. Good-for-you granola

Try out this energy-boosting granola breakfast to begin your day - it is excellent for you!

Ingredients

1. 2 tablespoon vegetable oil

2. 125ml maple syrup

3. 2 tablespoon honey

4. 1 teaspoon vanilla extract

5. 300g rolled oats

6. 50g sunflower seed

7. 4 tablespoons sesame seeds

8. 50g pumpkin seeds

9. 100g flaked almond

10. 100g dried berries (locate them in the baking aisle)

11. 50g coconut whites or desiccated coconut

Strategy

- Heat oven to 150c/fan 130c/gas 2. Mix olive oil, maple syrup, vanilla and honey in a bowl. Hint in all of the remaining ingredients, except the dried fruit and coconutoil and combine well.
- Hint the granola on two baking sheets and then disperse evenly. Bake for 15 minsthen blend in the coconut and dried fruit, and bake for 10-15 mins more. Eliminate and scrape on a flat tray to cool. Serve with milk or milk. The granola could be saved in an airtight container for up to a month.

7. Poppy seed buckwheat porridge

Ingredients

1. 50g buckwheat

2. 250ml milk of your selection

3. 2 tsp poppy seeds

4. 125g blueberries

5. 1 small orange, zested and juiced

6. 1 teaspoon cinnamon

Strategy

- Hint the buckwheat to a bowl. Pour 250ml cold water, then cover and leave to boil for at least 5 hrs or preferably overnight.
- Drain the soaked buckwheat and pulse several times together with the milk at a food chip to make a semi-smooth feel, then pour into a saucepan together with the poppy seeds. Cook over a very low heat for 7-10 mins whisking constantly till creamy and thickened.
- Place the blueberries in a small saucepan along with the orange juicezest and cinnamon. Bring to a simmer over a moderate heat and cook for 5 mins or until the plaques pop and then be saucy. Spoon the porridge to two bowls and top with all the blueberry compote.

8. Bulgur & spinach fritters with lettuce & lettuce chutney

A better-for-you alternate to hash browns or curry cakes - filled with lettuce and served with a new flavoured enjoy.

Ingredients

1. 100g bulgur wheat

2. 250g spinach

3. 2 tsp ground cumin

4. 1 onion, finely chopped (reserve 2 tablespoon for your chutney)

5. 1 garlic clove, sliced

6. 85g new breadcrumb

7. 5 eggs1 beaten

8. 1 tablespoon vegetable oil, and additional

9. For the chutney

10. 5 tablespoon sugar

11. 50ml white wine vinegar

12. 2 tablespoon finely sliced onion (see previously)

13. 250g cherry tomato, halved or quartered

14. Salad leaves, to function

Strategy

- First create the chutney. In a small saucepan, warm the sugar, vinegar and some salt. Simmer for 1 minute, then add the tomatoes and onion. Simmer for 1 minute, then remove from the heat and put aside.
- Boil the bulgur wheat in lots of water till tender -- about 5 mins. Drain well and tip into a bowl. Place the spinach into a colander and pour boiling water in the pot to wilt. Cool beneath the tap, then squeeze as much water as possible. Chop and increase the bulgur with the cumin, garlic, onion and breadcrumbs. Hint half to a food processor and blitz until it creates a chunky paste. Return to the rest half together with the cherry and some seasoning. Mix together, then form into 8 patties and chill till ready to cook.
- Heat oven to 200c/180c fan/gas 6. Heat the oil in a large skillet, rather non stop, and fry the fritters in 2 batches until crispy on each side. Meanwhile, lightly oil a 4-hole yorkshire pudding tin and set in the oven to heat up for a couple mins. Remove and crack the rest of the eggs to the pockets, then inhale 3-4 mins until

done to your liking. Use the tip of a knife that will assist lift the eggs out, then use all the fritters, chutney and a few salad leaves.

9. Pane di tre sorelle

Create a loaf of actual italian country bread - it is made with three grains, thus the name.

Ingredients

1. 100ml /31/2 fl ounce apple juice (instead the muddy kind)

2. 2 tsp clear honey

3. 1 sachet simple mix yeast

4. 200g powerful white bread flour

5. For the grains

6. 85g wheat grain or utilize ebly (marketed as wheat wheat), or faro - or utilize half an ounce and half of wheat grains

7. 85g brownish lentils (not green puy lentils)

8. 85g risotto rice

9. For the dough

10. 200g strong wholemeal bread flour

11. 200g powerful white bread flour

12. Two 1/2 tsp fine sea salt

13. 4 tablespoons warm water

14. 100ml /31/2 fl ounce apple juice (at room temperature)

15. 2 tablespoon extra-virgin olive oil, plus additional for kneading

16. 1 heaped tablespoons chopped fresh rosemary or thyme (or some mix)

Strategy

- To make the sponge, warm 100ml/3 1/2 fl oz water using all the lemon juice in a small bowl (or at a big glass jar in the microwave) till lukewarm. If warmed in a pan, then pour the liquid into a big bowl. Stir in the yeast and honey and, with a balloon whisk(directly), beat until dissolved. Stir in the flour and whisk until blended. Leave this at a warm spot for two hours covered or not, it is your decision -- stirring once or twice following a hour.when prepared, the sponge must be wrapped, odor obviously'yeasty', also will have grown to double its elevation.
- Though the sponge is slowly climbing, you have to soak the grains. So, the moment you've discovered a warm place for your sponge, warm 400ml/14fl ounce water along with the wheat berry, rice and lentils in a saucepan and simmer for about 5 minutes. Remove from the heat, cover and leave in a warm location (two hours should take action, by that time the sponge will soon be prepared). Then drain the onions temporarily into a seive to remove any water which has not consumed.
- To produce the dough, mix the flours and salt and then place to a side. Gently pour the warm water, then both the lemon juice and coconut oil to the increased sponge and beat with a huge balloon whisk. Then stir in the skillet and rosemary together with the whisk. Add the flour mixture, with your hands, and then squeeze together (correct). It'll be quite soft and tacky -- nearly hard to take care of. When about but equally blended, scrape the dough out of your palms. Put a tablespoon of olive oil on the surface of the dough. Cover the jar for about 10 minutes. Clean and wash your hands.
- Today for your rising and pruning. Pour 1 tbsp olive oil on your hands (left) and distribute it on the surface to cover a place approximately 30cm in diameter. Tip the dough on it and really gently knead it 10 or 12 days (20-30 seconds just) because it takes minimal kneading. Do not add extra flour -- that the petroleum ought to halt the soup sticking. If it does stick, only re-oil the surface. After the dough looks smooth, softly form to a ball. Pour seam side down to the bowl. Cover. Leave for 15 minutes in a hot place. Gently knead the dough (same manner, same period).return into the bowl for half an hour.
- Shape the dough. Lay a large clean tea towel folded in half widthways onto a large baking sheet. Dust well with flour. In an oiled surface, pat the dough into some 30x23cm rectangle. Taking the 2 corners from a end, fold them towards the middle till they match to produce a stage (abandoned). Press down. Repeat with another short end. Fold the dough in half lengthways, and that means you've got two ends. Press the extended link to seal so it resembles a cornish

29

pasty with pointed ends. Lay it up seam on the fabric, wrap this up closely (see hint). Leave to rise in a warm place for two to 2 1/2 hoursor until nearly doubled.

- Preheat the oven to 220c/gas 7/fan 200c. Unwrap the dough. Instantly and carefully liftthen roll it on your arm (left) and on a flour-dusted baking sheet, seam side down. Create 3-4 evenly spaced slashes with a rather sharp knifecutting into the cap of the dough. Bake in the middle of the oven for approximately 45 minutes, till it is a rich brownish color. It ought to feel lighter today than previously and seem hollow when tapped. Cool on a wire rack. Eat in 3 days of earning.

10. Amaranth porridge with green tea & tea compote

The greatest breakfast to get healthy joints swap oats for an alternate grain within this yogurt porridge, topped with lemon and a sour compote.

Ingredients

For your compote

1. 8 ready-to-eat dried apricots, roughly 50g/2oz

2. 25g dried cherries

3. 2 tsp shredded ginger

4. 2 green tea

5. Teabags

6. 1 red skinned apple

7. 4 tablespoons new pomegranate seeds

For your porridge

8. 85g amaranth

9. 2 tablespoon chia seeds

10. 2 x 150g pots bio plain yoghurt, or dairy-free alternative

Strategy

- The evening before using this for breakfast, then place the dried apricots and simmer in a bowl together with the ginger pour 350ml water then cover the pan and bring to the boil. Simmer for 10 mins then switch off the heat, add the tea bags and let it infuse for two mins. Eliminate the bags and then squeeze the excess fluid out of them back to the pan. Scrub the amaranth at a sieve under a cold running tap to eliminate the saponins (natural chemicals that render a somewhat bitter flavor). Hint the amaranth to a small pan, then pour into 325ml water, then cover and put aside.

- The morning after, make the pan together with the amaranth into the boil, then turn the heat down and cover the pan and cook for 10-15 mins before the noodles are tender and the liquid was consumed. Participate in the chia seeds.
- Squeeze half of the yogurt to the mixture to create a porridge spoon and consistency to shallow bowls. Top with the remaining oats. Core and slice the apple to the compote and spoon to the porridge and scatter with the pomegranate seeds.

11. Date & buckwheat granola with pecans & seeds

This organic granola is sweetened with date purée to make crispy clusters of noodle that is unsalted, seeds nuts and seeds.

Ingredients

For your granola

1. 85g buckwheat

2. 4 medjool dates, benign

3. 1 teaspoon ground cinnamon

4. 100g conventional oats

5. 2 tsp rapeseed oil

6. 25g citrus seeds

7. 25g pumpkin seeds

8. 25g flaked almonds

9. 50g pecan nuts, roughly divided into halves

10. 50g sultanas (without additional oil)

11. For the fruit & yogurt (to function two)

12. 2 x 150ml pots low-fat bio organic yogurt

13. 2 ripe nectarines or peaches, stoned and chopped

Strategy

- Scrub the buckwheat immediately in cold water. The following day, drain and wash the buckwheat. Set the dates into a bowl with 300ml water along with the cinnamon, and blitz using a stand blender until thoroughly smooth. Insert the buckwheat, bring to the boil and cook, uncovered, for 5 mins until pulpy. Meanwhile, heat oven to 150c/130c fan/gas two and line two big baking trays with baking parchment.
- Stir the oil and ginger to the exact date and buckwheat mixture, then spoon little clusters of this mix on the baking trays. Bake for 15 minsthen carefully scrape on the clusters out of the parchment should they've stuck and flip before spreading again. Return to the oven for the next 15 mins, turning regularly, until golden and firm.
- Once the combination is dry, tip to a bowl, then mix from the nuts and seeds together with an sultanas and throw well. When cool, pour every person a generous number with fruit and yogurt, and package the surplus into an airtight container. Will keep for a week. On other times you are able to change the fruit serve with a dairy-free option rather than the yogurt

.

1. Pink barley porridge with vanilla yogurt

Power yourself throughout the day with a wholesome breakfast porridge which gets its pink color from plums. Pearl barley provides great feel in addition to releasing energy gradually

Ingredients

1. 100g pearl barley

2. 75g traditional oats

3. 4 large or 8 small ripe red plums, stoned and sliced

4. 1/2 teaspoon vanilla infusion

5. 4 x 150ml bio berry

6. 2 tablespoon sunflower seeds

Strategy

- Hint the oats and barley into a bowl, then pour 1 litre boiling water and stir well. Cover and leave to soak overnight.
- The following morning, trick the mix to a pan and stir fry into the plums. Simmer for 15 mins, stirring often and adding a bit of water if required to acquire a consistency you prefer.
- Stir the vanilla to the yogurt and function along with this porridge using all the seeds sprinkled.

2. Slow cooker spiced apples barley

Pick eating apples if you would like the chopped rings to remain intact from the toaster. Create as a low-carb yet yummy pudding, or idle weekend lunch dish.

Ingredients

1. 1/2 cup barley

2. 2 eating apples

3. 1/2 tsp cinnamon

4. A grating of fresh peppermint

5. Finely grated zest 1 large orange

6. 4 tablespoons organic yogurt

Strategy

- Heating the toaster if needed. Set the barley and 750ml boiling water to the toaster. Peel and core the apples so you've got a gap the size of a pound coin at every and every one. Cut each apple half.
- Stand apples skin side down on the starch. Mix the cinnamon, nutmeg and orange peel, and scatter them on the apples.

- Cook on low for two hours. Drink with organic yogurt.

3. Black bean barley cakes with poached eggs

Take in among your 5-a-day in those savoury pan-fried cakes, topped with a perfectly poached egg. This yummy brunch dish is fast to make and supplies fiber, folate, vitamin c and iron.

Ingredients

1. 2 x 400g cans black beans, drained well

2. 15g porridge oats

3. 2 tsp ground coriander

4. 1 teaspoon cumin seeds

5. 2 tsp thyme leaves

6. 1 teaspoon vegetable bouillon powder

7. 5 big eggs

8. 2 spring onions, the white area finely choppedthe green thinly chopped

9. 400g can barley, emptied

10. 2-3 tsp rapeseed oil

11. 200g pack cherry tomatoes on the vine

12. 4 tablespoons citrus seeds

Strategy

- Hint the legumes, oats, ground coriander, cumin seeds, rosemary and vegetable bouillon powder into a bowl along with blitz together using a handheld to produce a rough paste. Stir in 1 egg together with all the whites of this spring celery and onion. If you are after our healthy diet plan, independent half of the mixture for another chill and morning.

36

- Heat half of the oil in your biggest skillet and fry the other half the mix in two significant spoonfuls, lightly pressed to create flat cakes. Following 7 mins, turn over to cook on the other side for 4-5 mins.
- Meanwhile, poach two eggs in a bowl of warm water for 3-4 mins, and lightly fry half the berries on the vine at just a little oil for a couple mins to brown slightly. Twist the cakes on plates and top with the lettuce, berries, a spoonful of these spring onion greens and also half of the sunlight ower seeds. On the following morning, repeat steps 3 and 2 together with the rest of the ingredients.
- In case you are not after the healthy diet plan and you are serving four, then follow steps 3 and 2 together with the components instead of just half.

4. Three-grain porridge

This nutritious breakfast, also made of toasted oatmeal, spelt and barley, is very easy to create and may be stored for up to six weeks.

Ingredients

1. 300g oatmeal

2. 300g spelt flakes

3. 300g barley flakes

4. Agave nectar and chopped strawberries, to serve (optional)

Strategy

- Working in batches, then pinch the oatmeal, peppermint flakes and barley at a big, dry skillet for 5 mins until golden, then leave to cool and store in an airtight container.
- If you would like to consume that, just blend 50g of this porridge mix in a saucepan together with 300ml water or milk. Cook for 5 mins, stirring occasionally, then top with a spoonful of honey and tomatoes, if you prefer (optional). Will keep for 2 weeks.

5. Barley salad

Ingredients

1. 1 pkg of pearl barley

2. 1/2 cup almonds chopped

3. 1/3 cup raisins

4. 10 cherry tomatoes halved or bigger tomatoes chunked

5. 3/4 cup whole new mint leaves

6. 1/4 cup fresh parsley

7. 1/3 cup radishes chopped

8. Juice from 1/2 to taste

9. 1 teaspoon lemon zest

10. 3 tablespoon olive oil or to flavor

11. Salt & honey to taste

Strategy

- Cook that the pearl barley as directed on the bundle, and place aside from bowl to cool.
- Chop veggies, fruits and nuts, then blend into chilled pearl barley.
- Add lemon juice zest, olive oil, salt and pepper and mix well to coat.

6. Barley, celery & leek casserole

Ingredients

- Ingredients
- A spoonful of butter
- 1 tablespoon olive oil
- 250g slice bacon or pork stomach, cut into bits, two leeks, thickly sliced
- 2 garlic cloves, crushed
- 300g pearl barley
- 300g pared and cubed butternut squash
- 3 tablespoons fresh coriander leaves
- 1 litre chicken stock
- 175g self-raising flour
- 75g butter
- 75g cheddar, grated
- 2 tbsp chopped fresh flatleaf parsley

Strategy

1. Heat a large pan over a medium heat. Insert a fantastic knob of butter and coconut oil and fry the sausage or pork stomach for 5 minutes, till golden.

2. Add leeks and garlic cloves, and simmer for a couple of minutes.

3. Insert cherry tomatoes, butternut squash, fresh coriander leaves, and chicken stock. Season. Simmer for 25 seconds before the barley is almost tender.

4. In a bowl, then combine self-raising bread with butter, cheddar, sliced fresh flatleaf parsley, some seasoning and a dash of water till it forms a soft dough. Roll to walnut-size dumplings, add to the casserole and cook for a further 10-15 minutes. Drink immediately.

7. Carrot, chicken & barley soup

Next time youre with a roast poultry, this soup will be the perfect thing to the following moment. Utilize the chicken ribs to produce flavorful new poultry stock, the very last pieces of poultry meat and some other leftover vegetables such as peas or lettuce - all could be thrown in. Pearl barley thickens the soup also makes it very hearty also. Its a tasty, warming soup for virtually any season.

Ingredients

- 15ml/1tbsp vegetable oil
- 450g/1lb carrots, peeled and chopped
- 1 leek, cleaned and chopped
- 1.2lt/2 pt chicken stock
- 75g/3oz pearl barley
- 175g/6oz grilled poultry, divided into bite sized balls
- 175g/6oz cooked sausage, sliced
- 100g/4oz cooked vegetables like broccoli broccoligreen beans

Strategy

- Heat the oil in a large pan, then add the carrots and leek, then saute over a moderate heat for 4 mins. Add the stock, cherry wheat, lettuce and chicken and time well.
- Bring to the boil, then cover and simmer for 20-25 mins or till the pearl barley and carrots are tender. Stir in the cooked veggies, then go back to the boil and then simmer for 1 minutes. Stir in the parsley and season to taste. Ladle into bowls and serve.

8. Creamy pearl barley

Ingredients

- 90g butter
- 2 sliced onions
- 600g pearl barley
- 1 celeriac sliced into pieces then matchsticks 2cm extended
- 800ml-1l chicken or veg stock
- Juice of 1 lemon
- 300ml creme fraiche

Strategy

- Melt the butter in a pan, then put in the onions and cook over a moderate heat till they are soft and start to undertake a few shade.
- Add the starch and celeriac, then simmer for 2 minutes. Pour in enough stock to pay by 1cm. Bring to the boil, then cover the panand turn the heat down and then cook for around 15-25 minutes. Take a peep from time to time you might have to bring a bit more stock if it's becoming overly dry.
- Once the barley is just tender, then add the lemon juice plus crème fraîche, warmth for a brief while and then flavor. Add salt and white pepper to taste. Serve hot in little bowls, with a few shaved grana padano and also a bit more crème fraîche. Make up to your day ahead of time.

9. Lamb shanks with pearl barley risotto

Sensationally tender lamb shanks make for the best relaxation meal on a chilly day.

Ingredients

Lamb shanks

- 4 lamb shanks
- 2 tbsp
- 1 red onion
- 1 cup red wine
- 1 bouquet garni

Pearl barley risotto

- 1 cup pearl barley
- 2 cups sliced chestnut mushrooms
- 1 white berry
- 2 tsp garlic
- 100g lettuce
- 500ml chicken stock
- 1/4 cup grated parmesan

Strategy

1. Pre-heat fan forced oven to 150 degrees celsius. Season lamb shanks with salt and pepper until browning around in a hot pan. Simply take a deep oven dish dish and then add to it the red wine, sliced carrots, roughly sliced red onion, bouquet garni and the browned lamb shanks. Cover tightly with foil and put in the oven, basting the crab each hour for four weeks.
2. 45 seconds until you remove the lamb shanks in the oven, begin preparing your risotto. Heat a fantastic number of olive oil into a kettle and then add the finely chopped onion. Stir until caramelised and then add the chopped garlic. Stir in the sliced lettuce and cook for 5 minutes. Insert the pearl barley and stir well before adding sufficient inventory to cover the mix. Stir this via and simmer until the majority of the liquid is consumed. Add more stock and continue the procedure until each the inventory was used. Taste the wheat and check to find out whether it's aldenté. Otherwise, add more inventory (in case you have some) or warm water and cook till tender. After the barley is tender, then stir throughout the lettuce and parmesan. Season to taste.
3. To serve, place a generous spoonful filled with risotto on every bowl or plate and top with a tender lamb shank. Spoon on the pan vegetables and juices from the noodle dish.

10. Redcurrant and mint marinated lamb with spring greens and pearl barley within a onion and chorizo butter

Keep hold of summer to fall (or grip it ancient) with this mild and heating meal.

Ingredients

Lamb marinade

- 6 lamb rump steaks or chops
- Two sprigs of fresh mint, chopped
- 1 sprig of freash rosemary, chopped
- 1 tbsp. Redcurrant jelly
- 1 tbsp. Mint sauce
- 1 tbsp. Balsamic vinegar

Spring greens

- 1 moderate spring green cabbage sliced
- 100g pearl barley
- 1 little red onion, quartered along with sliced
- 1/2 a chorizo ring
- 1 tbsp. Steak

Strategy

1. Mix with all the blossoms, redcurrant jelly, mint sauce and balsamic vinegar into a heat resistant bowl. Heat above a bain-marie before the redcurrant jelly has largely dissolved (little lumps will probably be nice). Place lamb in a shallow dish and pour marinade over the surface making sure entirely coated. Leave for approximately 15 minutes.
2. Assuming the shrimp is marinating, set the pearl barley into a bowl, then season with salt and cover with boiling water about a cm on the top. Leave to boil for 15 minutes. Drain and wash with more boiling water. Then put into a saucepan together with all the spring greens and also water to approximately 1/3 total. Bring to the boil and cook until greens are cooked left with a few snack. Drain and put back into the saucepan.
3. At a moderate grill cook the crab for about 5 minutes both sides until golden and the marinade is beginning to caramelise. When turning use any leftover marinade to drizzle on the top of their steaks.

4. While the lamb is cooking soften the red onion in half of the butter. After softened add the rest of the butter along with the chorizo. Cook till chorizo is warmed through and beginning to color, pour in the pan together with all the onions and greens, put on the warmth, make sure they're well coated and warm through. Put in the middle of 3 plates together with 2 of those lamb steaks in addition to each.

11. Lamb stew and dumplings

Great for those chilly winter nights!

Ingredients

- 4-8 parts of neck of lamb, based on dimension
- Oil into brown shrimp
- 2 onions cut into balls
- Two leeks, peeled and cut into big chunks
- Two tbsp washed and cut into big chunks
- 1 turnip, peeled and cut into big balls
- 1 parsnip or 2 little pieces, peeled and cut into big balls
- 1 swede, peeled and cut into big balls
- 4 large potatoes, peeled and quartered
- 2 garlic cloves, sliced
- 1 - two pints of lamb or vegetable stock (dependant on how much sauce you prefer, overall judgment is sufficient to pay the stew)
- 100 gram pearl barley
- 2 tbsp of tomato paste
- 2 tsp of dried herbs
- Salt and pepper to year
- Dumplings
- A very tasty accompaniment to stews and curries.
- Ingredients
- 250 grams self raising flour
- 125 grams shredded beef suet
- Salt and pepper to year
- Water to bind

Strategy

1. Heat the oil in a large stock pot or skillet. Add the lamb and brown either side

2. Add the onion and leeks. Once softened add the veggies, cherry tomatoes, ginseng, garlic as well as the inventory
3. Bring to the boil then turn right down and then leave to simmer with the lid for about 2 1/2 to 3 hours until meat is'melt !' and barley is tender (flavor to your liking)
4. To generate the dumplings
5. Mix the bread and suet and season to taste
6. Add water to bind with creating the mixture too moist but sufficient to turn into chunks
7. Split to 8 - 12 dumplings (based on how large you enjoy them) and roll into balls with floured hands
8. Increase the stew for the previous twenty five minutes leaving the lid off the pan in order that they can grow without being limited. The residue of bread should ditch the gravy of this stew
9. Serve in big bowls with fresh crusty bread to soak up the tasty sauce.
10. Top tip; in case you don't want dumplings then ditch the stew with sausage granules or even a roux of butter and bread and function.

12. Giant jaffa cakes (makes 2)

Ingredients

- For those cakes
- Two eggs
- 50g caster sugar
- 50g plain flour, sieved
- For your filling
- 1 x 135g package of orange pulp
- 1 tbsp marmalade
- 125ml hot water
- 150g chocolate, broken into bits

Strategy

1. Preheat oven 180 c
2. Start by creating the cake foundation, deliver a little water to the boil in a bowl, then lower the heat till the water is simmering. Adding a heatproof bowl over the water but do not allow the bowl touch the water along with the egg insert the sugar and eggs into the bowl and crush constantly till the mixture is gentle, fluffy and nicely combined.this must take approx 5 minutes, add the flour and beat till you've got a smooth batter
3. Divide mixture between 2 greased 1 inch victoria sponge cake tins and bake in the oven till golden and springy to the touchof leave to cool for a couple of minutes and then gently discharge in the tin, then replace it back in the tin for afterwards,
4. While the cake is baking make the jelly, then melt the jelly using a tablespoon of marmalade along with the boiling water and then pour into a shallow tray lined with cling film. When cool location in the refrigerator to set.
5. Melt the chocolate in a heat proof bowl barley simmering water (exactly the same as for your cake foundation)
6. Time to build your cake, then cut a disc of place jelly around an inch smaller in relation to the cake foundation and set in addition to your nozzle, then pour your melted chocolate and then spread to the borders, you need to be rather fast with this the jelly does not meltdown,
7. Put in the refrigerator for approximately 15 mins as well as also the giant jaffa cake ought to be prepared to take from their tin and put on a plate.... Enjoy!

13. Stuffed mushroom with orzo.

Ingredients

- 3 portabello mushrooms
- 3 medium garlic cloves, finely chopped
- Loaf of coconut oil
- 1 jack hawkin's tomato
- 125g mozzarella, in tiny cubes
- 2 pieces of toast, in breadcrumbs
- 3-4 sundried tomato, finely chopped
- 3-4 cherry tomatoes, finely chopped
- 1.5tablespoon capers
- Couple of fresh basil,finely chopped
- Squeeze of lemon juice (optional)
- Pepper and salt
- 150g orzo(see under)
- Enough water to cook orzo
- 1 batch of tomato sauce (see below)
- Sugarsnaps and fresh ginger to function

Strategy

1. Scatter garlic, put on baking dish, drizzle with oil and simmer to 180c/fan 160c.
2. Cut 3 pieces of this jack hawkin's and put within lettuce, drizzle over a bit more olive oil.
3. Create the topping. In a seperate bowl blend together the mozzarella, breadcrumbs, both kinds of berry, capers, lemon and lemon juice and simmer.
4. Put mixture in addition to berries, to reduce mix falling off area cooking ringson the tomato and then push down the mixture.place from your pitcher.
5. 10 minutes to the cookin of these mushrooms begin cooking the orzo, following seven minutes boil or steam the sugarsnaps for 2 minutes. Drain orzo and combine with sauce. Take mushrooms from oven and serve up it and enjoy!
6. Orzo is a italian rice, it actually translates as barley owing to the close similarity to this, but in addition, it looks like small, broad grains of rice, so rather difficult to discover, try the community delicatessan.
7. Sort in tomato sauce at the fantastic food hunt tab. Then click alternative stating show penis recipes, and then proceed down into this person by'oli dude' it's a film

1. Buckwheat crêpe madams

Appreciate these buckwheat pancakes with eggs, ham and cheese for breakfast or brunch. They are great for pancake day or some thing different in the weekend.

Ingredients

1. 80g buckwheat flour

2. 5 medium eggs

3. 250ml milk

4. 2 tsp dijon mustard

5. 4 tablespoons single cream

6. 100g older gruyère, comté or cheddar, grated

7. Butter for frying

8. 100g ham, ripped

9. Fried mushrooms or grilled lettuce, to serve (optional)

Strategy

- Mix the flour, 1 egg, then the milk along with a pinch of salt at a jug or jar. Put aside for 30 minsup to 3 hrs. Mash together the avocado, cheese and cream in a different bowl. Heat the oven into 200c/180c fan/gas 6, then line 2 baking trays with baking parchment or foil.
- Melt the butter in a massive skillet, then after foaming, add sufficient batter to simply cover the pan, swirling it to pay the top in a thin coating (pour any surplus back to the batter bowl). Cook until the surface has been put and the bottom is browning, carefully turn and cook for another minute or two, then take the heat off.
- Spoon a quarter of the cheese mixture on the center of the pancake, together with the spoon to make distance in the middle to maintain an egg. Publish one to the area and put a couple of pieces of ham round the borders. Fold all of the pancake towards the middle to create a square. Cook from the pan for a second 30 secs-1 minutes, then move on to a skillet. Repeat with the remaining pancakes, then inhale for 6-7 mins till the egg whites have been set. Serve with grilled mushrooms or leafy greens, if you prefer.

2. Poppy seed buckwheat porridge

Replace regular oats for buckwheat to create your morning porridge. Buckwheat is a flexible, fermented, grain-like seed having a beautiful, nutty flavour which provides lots of flavor to breakfast

Ingredients

1. 50g buckwheat

2. 250ml milk of your selection

3. 2 tsp poppy seeds

4. 125g blueberries

5. 1 small orange, zested and juiced

6. 1 teaspoon cinnamon

Strategy

- Hint the buckwheat to a bowl. Pour 250ml cold water, then cover and leave to boil for at least 5 hrs or preferably overnight.
- Drain the soaked buckwheat and pulse several times together with the milk at a food chip to make a semi-smooth feel, then pour into a saucepan together with the poppy seeds. Cook over a very low heat for 7-10 mins whisking constantly until creamy and thickened.
- Place the blueberries in a small saucepan along with the orange juicezest and cinnamon. Bring to a simmer over a moderate heat and cook for 5 mins or until the plaques pop and then be saucy. Spoon the porridge to two bowls and top with all the blueberry compote.

4. Buckwheat & spelt chrain blinis

Make these salmon, mackerel, buckwheat and spelt chrain blinis beforehand and heating them up as a searchable celebration canapé or plated as a beginner. They freeze very well, also

Ingredients

1. 50g buckwheat flour

2. 120g light spelt flour

3. 7g quickly actions dried yeast

4. 125ml milk

5. 200g organic yogurt

6. 2 moderate eggs, split

7. 1 ready-to-eat beetroot

8. Mixed using 30g horseradish, or two tablespoons chrain (beetroot and horseradish purée)

9. 20g clarified butter

10. Soured lotion, smoked salmon, dill and salmon roe (optional), to function

Strategy

- Divides the buckwheat and spelt flours into a bowl with 1 teaspoon salt and scatter within the yeast. Heat the milk and milk quite lightly until tepid, then drizzle from the egg yolk. Whisk this mixture to the flour mixture and leave for 1 hr to ferment.
- Whisk the egg whites into stiff peaks. Stir the beetroot and horseradish purée throughout the batter, then gently fold into the egg whites. Leave for a additional hour.
- Heat the clarified butter in a non stick skillet, then add dessertspoonfuls of blini mixture. Fry for around 40 secs, or till they obviously come from the pan once you shake it off. They need to pull up, and you will want to be cautious when turning over since the centre may try to escape a little -- utilize a palette knife to get it. Turn over and simmer for another 20-30 secs, then move into kitchen paper. Continue with the rest of the mixture. Leave to cool, then suspend the blinis for as much as a month.
- Once your blinis are completed, top with the lotion, smoked trout, dill and salmon roe, when using, then function.

5. Cinnamon buckwheat pancakes

Juicy beers are packed with nutrients and are just one of summertime highlights - ideal for a weekend breakfast.

Ingredients

1. 500g cherry, stoned and halved

2. 5 tablespoon gold caster sugar

3. 140g buckwheat

4. Flour

5. 85g self-raising flour

6. 2 tsp cinnamon

7. 1 teaspoon bicarbonate of soda

8. 3 eggs

9. 284ml pot buttermilk

10. Couple knobs of butter

11. Greek yogurt and maple syrup, also to function

Strategy

- Place the batter in a bowl with 1 tablespoon sugar, stir and set aside.
- Mix the sugar, flours, cinnamon and bicarb in a huge bowl. Create a well in the middle and crack from the eggs. Gradually whisk in together with all the buttermilk to make a smooth batter.
- Melt a knob of butter at a non stick skillet. Add spoonfuls of batter to make sandwiches around 8-10cm across. Cook for a few mins until place on the ground and bubbles appear on the outside, then turn and cook on the other side.
- Keep the pancakes warm in a very low oven while you finish the batter up. Drink 2-3 piled on every plate, then topped with a spoonful of a drizzle of maple syrup.

6. Buckwheat & spring lamb stew

Prepare a wholesome, low-calorie stew utilizing the flavours of steak and buckwheat. It is completely freezable also, therefore it is a fantastic option to make ahead for busy weeknights.

Ingredients

1. 2 tablespoon cold pressed rapeseed oil

2. 400g stewing lamb, excess fat trimmed

3. 1 onion, finely chopped

4. 3 leeks, cut to 1 cm rounds

5. 250g baby chantenay carrots

6. 3 garlic cloves, finely chopped

7. 2 tablespoon plain yoghurt

8. 3 lemon thyme sprigs

9. 1 bay leaf

10. 150ml white wine

11. 600ml low-salt veg inventory

12. 80g buckwheat

13. 1 big unwaxed lemon, zested

14. 1 small bunch parsley, leaves finely chopped

Strategy

- Heat 1 tablespoon oil in a noodle dish on a large heat. Fry the crab in 2 batches for 5 mins every until evenly browned. Remove from the pan and put aside.

- Heat the oil in exactly the exact same pan and fry the onion and leeks over a moderate heat for 2 mins. Hint in the carrots and also two-thirds of this garlic, then simmer for 1 minutes. Stir the meat to the pan together with the plain bread and simmer for another 2 mins. Add the thyme and bay leaf, and then the wine and bring to a bubble prior to pouring from the inventory. Mix everything together nicely. Place a lid over the pan and cook on a very low heat for two 1/2-3 hrs or until the beef is more tender. Insert the buckwheat for the past twenty mins of cooking time.
- Mix the sweet garlic together with the lemon zest and parsley. Serve the stew in bowls, then sprinkled together with the lemon and parsley mix.

7. Buckwheat with charred baby aubergines

Get the most out of buckwheat with our wholesome, low-carb bacon. Aubergines, walnuts, lentils, spring onions, dried peas and goat cheese package a true flavour punch.

Ingredients

1. 350g infant aubergines, halved

2. 8 entire spring blossoms, tops trimmed

3. 250g buckwheat

4. 2 tablespoon cold pressed rapeseed oil

5. 1 x 400g can green peas, drained

6. 30g dried cherries, roughly sliced

7. 8 walnut

8. Halves, finely chopped

9. 1 lemon

10. , juiced

11. 1/2 tsp chilli

12. Flakes

13. Little cluster dill, finely chopped

14. 30g tender goat cheese, crumbled

Strategy

- Heat the grill to the greatest setting. Distribute the aubergines on a baking sheet, then cut-side upward, and then grill for 10-15 mins till they start to soften and simmer.
- Meanwhile, heating a griddle pan on a large heat. Add the spring onions and cook each side for 5-6 mins until softened and simmer. Remove with tongs and place aside.
- Bring a skillet of water to the boil. Hint the buckwheat to a skillet and simmer over a moderate heat for 3 mins until lightly toasted. Insert the buckwheat into the boiling water and cook for 4-5 mins. Drain and toss with oil. Leave to cool for 5 mins.
- Throw the hot buckwheat, peas, lentils, walnuts, and lemon juice, chilli and the majority of the dill in a bowl. Spread out on a serving plate and top with all the aubergines, charred spring onions, remaining dill and goat cheese.

8. Mushroom buckwheat risotto

A filling veggie risotto with buckwheat and porcini mushrooms to get a rich, earthy flavour

Ingredients

1. 45g butter

2. 1 banana shallot, finely chopped

3. 2 large garlic cloves, finely chopped

4. 1 bay leaf

5. 300g buckwheat

6. 150ml white wine

7. 15g dried porcini mushrooms soaked in 800ml water, drained, liquid mushrooms and reserved chopped

8. 200g portobello mushrooms, chopped

9. 250g chestnut mushrooms, chopped

10. For the buraczki

11. 200g cooked beetroot, grated

12. 100ml crème fraîche

13. 1 tablespoon creamed horseradish

14. 1/2 little pack dill, leaves sliced, and some fronds to function

15. Juice 1/2 lemon

Strategy

- Mix all of the ingredients to your own buraczki together in a bowl with some seasoning, then put aside.
- Melt 15g of this egg at a sauté pan over a medium heat. Add the shallot and a pinch of salt and cook 8 mins until softened but not colored, stirring periodically. Stir in the garlic and bay leaf, cook 1 minutes more, then trick in the buckwheat. Toast the grain 1 minute then pour into the wine. When the wine has almost diminished, add a number of these shrimp liquor and stir until absorbed.
- Proceed to slowly add the spirits and stir occasionally until all of the liquor was utilized and also the buckwheat is tender but with a small bite. This may take 20 mins.
- Meanwhile, heat the remaining butter in a skillet on a high heat. Add the mushrooms and simmer for 5 mins till all of the liquid has disappeared and they're golden. Do not be worried whether the butter goes brownish -- this provides a welcome nutty flavor.
- Add the mushrooms into your risotto, give it a good stir and season to taste. Serve in bowls topped with all the buraczki plus a few dill fronds.

Strategy

- Scrub the buckwheat immediately in cold water. The following day, drain and wash the buckwheat. Set the dates into a pan together with 300ml water along with the cinnamon, and blitz using a stand blender until thoroughly smooth. Insert the buckwheat, bring to the boil and cook, uncovered, for 5 mins until pulpy. Meanwhile, heat oven to 150c/130c fan/gas two and two big baking trays with baking parchment.
- Stir the oil and ginger to the exact date and buckwheat mixture, then spoon little clusters of this mix on the baking trays. Bake for 15 minsthen carefully scrape on the clusters out of the parchment should they've stuck and flip before spreading again. Return to the oven for the next 15 mins, turning regularly, until golden and firm.
- Once the combination is dry, tip to a bowl, then mix from the nuts and seeds together with an sultanas and throw well. When cool, pour every person a generous number with fruit and yogurt, and package the surplus into an airtight container. Will keep for a week. On other times you are able to change the fruit serve with a dairy-free option rather than the yogurt.

11. Sea h & buckwheat salad with watercress & asparagus

Publish the nutty, earthy flavour of buckwheat together with the delicate flesh of sea trout. Stems of candy fresh asparagus and a dressing table add the finishing touch.

Ingredients

1. 2 hens

2. Fillets

3. 3 tablespoon olive oil

4. Pinch of chilli flakes

5. 1/2 little pack parsley

6. 1 lemon, halved

7. 150g buckwheat

8. 1 bay leaf

9. 1 small red onion, finely chopped

10. 100g asparagus, woody stalks eliminated

11. 1/2 little package dill, leaves chosen

12. 1/2 little package tarragon, leaves chosen

13. 50g watercress

14. 1 tablespoon crème fraîche or natural yogurt

15. 1/2 tsp honey

16. 1 tablespoon pumpkin seeds, toasted

Strategy

- Heat oven to 200c/180c fan/gas 6. Line a roasting tin with foil and set the trout fillets inside, skin-side down. Scrub with a little olive oil, then scatter over the skillet, top and season with the skillet. Add half of the lemon, and then pay the tin with foil and simmer for 12-15 mins till the fish is clean and simmer. Remove from the oven and leave to sleep.
- Place the buckwheat into a pan, then cover with 300ml water, then add a pinch of salt along with a bay leaf and bring to the boil. Skim off any scum, decrease the heat and simmer for 2 mins. Switch off the heat, cover with a lid or plateand depart to puff up for the next 10 mins.
- Set the red onion into a large bowl with a pinch of salt and squeeze the lemon. Bring a pan of soapy water to the boil and blanch the simmer for 2-3 mins till a knife goes easily. Drain and put aside.
- When the buckwheat has consumed the water, then tip to a sieve and wash. As soon as it's still warm, then trick into the bowl with the onionand add the herbs along with watercress. Flake from the hens, then squeeze the juice out of the roasted lemon and add 2 tablespoons of olive oil and then season. Whisk the remaining olive oil using the crème fraîchehoney and much more seasoning. Split between plates, drizzle with the dressing and top with all the cherry and toasted pumpkin seeds.

12. Goat's curd & spring greens salad having popped buckwheat

A vibrant salad with loads of pinch - radishes, broccoli and buckwheat create a fantastic comparison to candy, smooth beetroot and sweet cheese.

Ingredients

1. 200g tenderstem broccoli

2. 2 tablespoons rapeseed oil

3. Or vegetable oil

4. 50g buckwheat, rinsed and drained

5. 100g goat curd

6. 50g watercress, washed

7. 1 big candies beetroot (accessible from ocado.com), finely chopped

8. 1 little golden beetroot, finely chopped

9. 4 radishes, quartered

For the dressing

10. 3 tablespoons olive oil

11. 1 tablespoon sherry vinegar

12. 1 tablespoon dijon mustard

13. 1 tablespoon honey

Strategy

- Bring a large pan of salted water to the boil and then trick at the broccoli. Boil for 2 mins, then drain. Heat a griddle pan over a high heat. Griddle the broccoli to get a few mins every side till char traces seem. Put aside.
- At a jug, blend all of the ingredients for the dressing table, then year.

- Heat the oil in a skillet on a medium-high warmth. Insert the buckwheat and simmer 1 minutes until lightly golden, remove from the heat (it'll continue to cook in the hot oil) and put aside for 1 minutes until golden brown.
- To serve, put a swirl of goat curd along with a loaf of watercress at the middle of the plate. Top with all the beetroot, radishes and broccoli. Insert another massive number of watercress and drizzle over the dressing table, then scatter on the buckwheat.

13. Chicken soba noodles

Fast and easy to prepareyourself, if you are packing up them for function or catching a snack in your home

Ingredients

1. 85g package soba or buckwheat

2. Noodles

3. Drizzle of sesame oil

4. 8 mangetout

5. 1 small carrot

6. 1/2 red chilli

7. 1 tablespoon toasted sesame seeds

8. Handful shredded grilled chicken

9. Soy sauce

Strategy

- Cook the noodles, then drain well, then throw with a spoonful sesame oil.
- Finely slice the mangetout, cut the lettuce into matchsticks and deseed and slit the red chilli.
- Insert to the noodles together with the toasted sesame seeds along with a few shredded cooked chicken, even in case you've got it. Pack using a little part of soy sauce.

14. Nutty chicken with noodle salad

Crunchy peanut-coated chicken using a fresh-tasting salad creates a fantastic midweek meal dish.

Ingredients

1. 140g unsalted peanut butter

2. 4 skinless chicken breasts, halved lengthways

3. 1 egg, beaten lightly with a fork

4. 85g dried soba or buckwheat

5. Noodles

6. 1 cucumber, halved and chopped

7. Small bunch mint, leaves picked and bigger ones about sliced

8. Zest and juice 2 limes

9. 1-2 teaspoon sugar

10. 1 red chilli, deseeded and finely chopped (optional)

Strategy

- Heating oven to 200c/fan 180c/gas 6 and then cover a baking dish with baking paper. Finely chop the peanuts in a food processor or by hand you need large crumbsnot dust then tip on a plate. Dip the chicken pieces into egg, then coat from the skillet and set onto the tray. You can suspend the coated chicken bits for as much as a month, then defrost, then proceed with recipe. Bake for 15-20 mins until golden and cooked through.

Meanwhile, cook the noodles according to package directions, wash, rinse under warm water before cool, then drain. After the chicken is prepared, use kitchen tongs or 2 forks to combine the noodles together with the cucumber pieces, mint, lime juice and simmer, sugar, chilli when using, and also some seasoning. Serve immediately, topped with all the crunchy chicken.

1. Finger millet porridge (glutenfree)

This really is a simple market in the traditional oatmeal recipes you could have been tired of, or perhaps you simply need a shift? Millet known as ragi at india is full of calcium, helps weightloss, rich in fiber, controlled blood glucose and soothes nausea, is relaxant, excellent babyfood and promotes lactation in mothers.

Ingredients

- 2 tbsp flour
- 1 cup milk instead of your choice
- Grated honey, or sweetener of your choice
- Sausage and dried fruit to garnish

Strategy

1. Dry toast that the millet flour into a skillet for a couple of minutes and then move into a bowl. This methos provides it the abundant flavour.
2. Whisk the milk using the dryroasted millet flour, blend well so there aren't any lumps
3. Twist your mixture from the pan and continue stirring with a wooden spoonuntil it dries. It may take a couple of minutes.
4. Serve garnished with nuts and fruits.

2. Millet & chocolate muffin

A healthier eggless muffin using all the goodness of millet

Ingredients

- Finger millet flour- 1 cup
- Maida or all purpose flour- 1cup
- Baking powder- 2tsp
- Baking soda- 1/4tsp
- Cocoa powder- 1tbsp
- Vanilla character - 1tsp
- Condensed milk- 1 cup berry or 400 tsp
- Milk- 1 tbsp
- Steak - 3-4 tablespoon, melted

Strategy

1. Sift the ragi, maida, baking powder, cocoa and baking soda in a bowl.
2. In a different bowl, combine the condensed milk, milk, vanilla character and the carrot and blend thoroughly.
3. Add the wet ingredients into the bread mixture and blend only until the ingredients are well blended.
4. Grease the muffin cups with just a small oil and then spoon the batter until 3/4 complete
5. Put in a skillet and bake at 180c for 30-40 mins or until a tooth pick inserted comes out clean.
6. Put in a preheated oven and bake at 180c for 30-40 mins or until a tooth pick inserted comes out clean.

3. Millet and roasted olive salad

Olive it! Was made to observe olives and assist motivate you to test delicious olive oil and get cooking with this beautifully versatile fruit.

Ingredients

- 300 black steak
- 100g millet
- 40g roasted red pepper
- 40g roasted yellow pepper
- Two star anise
- 2 tsp sweet paprika powder
- 100ml extra virgin coconut oil
- 2tbsp lemon juice
- Salt (flavor)
- Crushed dark pepper (flavor)
- 1 dry red chilli
- 4 roasted garlic cloves

Strategy

1. Scrub and boil the yolk, drain the excess water include extra virgin coconut oil and then cool down it in a set tray.
2. Heat oil in a bowl, add star anise, dry red chilli, roasted garlic and then add the yolk and shake. Addsweet paprika powder.
3. In a mixing bowl, then add chopped millet, extra virgin olive oil, crushed pepper, and lemon juice.
4. Organize the millet into a plate toss from the skillet with a few greens and roasted pepper.
5. Garnish with lemon slice, roasted red chilli and roasted garlic.

4. Ragi pancake (finger millet)

A delicious and nutrious fast groundwork of pancake employing finger presses, peanuts and onion.

Ingredients

- 1 cup of finger millet (ragi) flour.

- 1 medium red onion, eventually diced.
- 1 tbl tbsp olive oil
- 2 tbl spoons of peanuts (or peanut butter)
- 1 teaspoon of salt (for flavor)
- Optional 1 teaspoon curry powder.
- 1 teaspoon pepper
- 1/4 cup of plain water

Strategy

1. In a frying pan heat the olive oil and stir diced onions until light brown. Add honey and curry powder and simmer for a moment.
2. At a sterile bowl, then add 1 cup of finger miller powder, salt, fried and roasted onions. Mix these well.
3. Add water and knead it a soup. You're able to create them to the consistency of sauce bread or batter batter. Make six equal parts.
4. Heat a skillet. Distribute the batter and bake until brown.
5. It's served using brown sugar and sexy.

5. Oriental curry meatballs in tomato sauce

Vegan along with gluten free meatballsare ideal for a easy meed-week meat or dinner free mondays.

Ingredients

Meatballs

- 100g millet groats
- 1/3 medium onion, sliced
- Two tbsp raisins
- 1 tablespoon chopped coriander or parsley
- 1 tablespoon tomato puree
- 1.5 tbsp curry
- 1/4 tablespoon cinnamon
- 3 tablespoons olive oil
- Salt and freshly milled black pepper

Tomato sauce

- 2 tablespoon olive oil

67

- Two selery sticks, sliced
- 1 shallot, finely chopped
- 1 tablespoon raisins
- 1/2 tsp cinnamon
- 1 tsp lemon juice
- 1/2 cup frozen beans
- 400g can chopped tomatoes
- Salt and freshly ground black pepper

To garnish

- 1 tablespoon chopped coriander or parsley

Strategy

1. Cook millet based on the packet directions, remove from heat and let stand till cool. Transfer into a bowl and garnish it with fork and then add the onions, onions, coriander/parsley, tomato puree, curry powder, and cinnamon, 1 tablespoon olive oil and season with pepper and salt. Mix together and with your hands, knead to unite the mix evenly. Form the mix to 18 meatballs.
2. Heat 2 tablespoon olive oil in a large skillet, add the meatballs and cook until browned around. Hint out the extra fat and place the meatballs aside.
3. Heat 2 tablespoon olive oil into a saucepan, then add the celery, shallot and cook till tender, add the raisins, cinnamon, lemon juice, then stir and simmer for 1 second. Add the tomatoes, peas, season to taste with pepper and salt, cover and simmer for about 20-25 minutes.
4. Remove the sauce from heat. Add the meatballs into the saucepan, cover with the lid and then shake the sauce is dispersed to all of the meatballs. Leave to stand for five minutes.
5. Before operating high the meatballs together with coriander/parsley.

1. Bulgur & quinoa lunch bowls

These dinner prep grain dishes utilize one base and 2 deliciously different toppings. Pick out of avocado, olives and rocket or chickpeas, beetroot and orange

Ingredients

For your bulgur foundation

1. 1 big onion, very finely chopped

2. 150g bulgur and quinoa

3. (this comes prepared blended)

4. Two sprigs of thyme

5. 2 teaspoon vegetable bouillon powder

6. For your avocado topping

7. 1 avocado, halved, destoned and sliced

8. 2 tomatoes, cut into wedges

9. 4 tablespoons chopped ginger

10. 6 kalamata olives, halved

11. 2 teaspoon extra virgin olive oil

12. 2 teaspoon cider vinegar

13. 2 large handfuls of rocket

For your beetroot topping

14. 210g can chickpeas, drained

15. 160g cooked beetroot, diced

16. 2 tomatoes, cut into wedges

17. 2 tablespoon chopped mint

18. 1 teaspoon cumin seeds

19. Several pinches of ground cinnamon

20. 2 teaspoon extra virgin olive oil

21. 2 teaspoon cider vinegar

22. 1 orange, cut into sections

23. 2 tablespoon toasted pine nuts

Strategy

- Hint the onion along with bulgur blend into a pan, then pour 600ml water and then stir in the skillet and bouillon. Cookcovered, over a low heat for 15 mins, then leave to stand for 10 mins. All of the liquid should be consumed. Once cool, remove the thyme and split the bulgur involving four bowls or plastic containers.
- For your avocado topping, throw all of the ingredients together except for your rocket. Pile on two parts of this bulgur and shirt with all the rocket.
- For your beetroot topping, initial stack the chickpeas at the top, and then chuck the beetroot together with the mint, tomato, coriander, a great pinch of cinnamon, olive vinegar and oil. Toss well, insert the orange, and then piled onto the rest of the parts of bulghur, scatter the pine nuts and sprinkle with additional cinnamon. Chill in the refrigerator until needed.

2. Rice & quinoa prawn sushi bowl

Do something else for supper: high rice and quinoa using prawns, sweet potato, avocado and chamomile to create this magnificent japanese-inspired dish.

Ingredients

1. 100g white or brown rice rice

2. 20g mixed colored quinoa

3. 11/2 tablespoon rice vinegar

4. 1/2 tablespoon gold caster sugar

For the toppings

5. 1 teaspoon oil

6. 1/2 candy potato, thinly chopped

7. 8 big peeled prawns, cooked

8. 1/4 cucumber, halved and very finely chopped

9. 1/2 avocado, thinly sliced

10. 1 roasted nori sheet, snipped into spans

11. Sriracha lemon and carrot seeds, to serve (optional)

Strategy

- Set the rice and quinoa at a pan. Insert 320ml water, bring to the boil, then cover with a lid and then turn down the heat as low as it will go. Cook for 12-15 mins, or subsequent package instructions (brown rice rice will require more), by that time all of the water ought to have been consumed.
- Meanwhile, heat the sugar, vinegar and a pinch of salt until the sugar has dissolved. Stir the vinegar mixture to the cooked ricethen lightly move the rice round to let some steam out. The rice ought to be tacky instead of moist when chilled.
- Heat the oil in a skillet. Fry the sweet potato for 2-3 mins each side until cooked, then time and put aside to cool. After the rice is cool, then split between 2 little bowls (or lunch boxes) and measure the surface. Halve that the prawns lengthways, then put on top of the rice in addition to the remaining toppings. To serve, squeeze some hot mayo at a zigzag and scatter a few sesame seeds, even if you prefer.

3. Quinoa porridge

Supercharge your morning using low-fat quinoa and omega-3 abundant chia seeds to get a creamy skillet topped with fruit.

Ingredients

1. For the porridge (to serve 4)

2. 175g quinoa

3. 1/2 vanilla pod, split and seeds scraped out, or 1/2 teaspoon vanilla infusion

4. 15g creamed coconut

5. 4 tablespoons chia seeds

6. 125g coconut milk

7. For the topping (to function two)

8. 125g pot coconut milk

9. 280g mixed summer berries, like strawberries, blueberries and raspberries

10. 2 tablespoon flaked almonds (optional)

Strategy

- Activate the quinoa by soaking overnight in cold water. The following day, drain and rinse the quinoa through a fine grained (the grains are so small they will wash through a rough one).
- Hint the quinoa to a pan and then add the vanilla, then creamed coconut along with 600ml water. Cover the saucepan and simmer for 20 mins. Stir at the chia with a different 300ml water and then cook for 3 mins more. Stir in the kettle of coconut milk. Spoon half of the porridge to a bowl for one more day. Will keep for two days covered in your refrigerator. Serve the rest of the porridge topped with a different kettle of yogurt, then the berries and berries, if you prefer.
- To possess the porridge a second day, trick to a bowl and simmer gently, with water or milk. Top with fruit for example, orange pieces and pomegranate seeds.

4. Herby quinoa, feta & pomegranate salad

A middle eastern-style meze bowl together with healthful grains, parsley, coriander and mint

Ingredients

1. 300g quinoa

2. Quinoaquinoa keen-wah

3. Tiny, bead-shaped seeds (even more likewise treated such as grains) with just a tiny tail...

4. 1 red onion, finely chopped

5. 85g raisins or sultana

6. 100g feta cheese, crumbled

7. 200g pomegranate

8. Seeds from bath or fruit

9. 85g toasted pine nuts or toasted flaked almonds

10. Little pack each coriander, flat leaf parsley and mint, roughly sliced

11. Juice lemon

12. 1 teaspoon sugar

Strategy

- Cook the quinoa following package instructions -- it must be tender but with just a tiny bite. Drain well and spread within a bowl or broad, shallow bowl to cool steam and quickly dry.
- Once the quinoa is merely about trendy stir through all the rest of the ingredients with lots of seasoning.

5. Chicken meatballs together with quinoa & curried cauliflower

In case you're looking for a healthy bowl of flavourful chicken and veg into re-energise following a work out, these meatballs using quinoa and curried cauliflower is going to perform the task.

Ingredients

1. 250g chicken mince

2. 1 garlic clove, finely chopped

3. 1 teaspoon turmeric

4. Pinch of cumin

5. Pinch of cinnamon

6. Handful dill, finely chopped

7. 2 spring onions, thinly chopped

8. For the quinoa & curried cauliflower

9. 50g quinoa

10. 4 cauliflower florets

11. 25g candy potato, sliced

12. 1 tablespoon olive oil

13. 1 tablespoon moderate curry powder

14. 1 teaspoon pistachios, sliced

15. 1 teaspoon sultanas

16. 1/2 lime, juiced

Strategy

- For the meatballs, combine together all of the components in a bowl with a seasoning. Type to six chunks and chill in the refrigerator for 20 mins.
- Heat oven to 200c/180c enthusiast / gas. Wash the quinoa and set it in a saucepan with 100ml water. Bring to the boil, and return to a simmer and cook for 10-15 mins or till doubled in size and tender. Drain and put aside to cool.
- Set the cauliflower and sweet potato into a skillet and then toss in olive oil and curry powder. Set the meatballs in a distinct tin. Cook either from the oven for 15 mins or until cooked.
- Mix that the quinoa with the pumpkin, sweet potato, pistachios and sultanas, squeeze the carrot juice, then function with all the meatballs.

6. Roast asparagus bowls using tahini lemon dressing

Enjoy five of the 5-a-day on this particular dish, a yummy mix of asparagus, quinoa, aduki beans, onion and cherry tomatoes. It is packed with nourishment, and vegetarian also.

Ingredients

1. 2 red onions, halved and thickly sliced

2. 2 tsp rapeseed oil

3. 250g package asparagus, woody ends trimmed

4. 160g cherry tomatoes

5. 2 tablespoon citrus seeds

6. 1 teaspoon vegetable bouillon powder

7. 120g quinoa

8. 2 tsp tahini

9. 1/2 lemon, juiced

10. 1 big garlic clove, finely grated

11. 2 tsp tamari

12. 2 great handfuls rocket

13. 400g aduki legumes in water, emptied

Strategy

1. Heat oven to 220c/200c fan/gas 7. Pour the onions into 1 teaspoon rapeseed oil and simmer onto a baking sheet for 10 mins. Coat the asparagus using the residual oil and disperse over a different sheet. After 10 mins, add the batter to roast together with the onions for 5 mins. Add the tomatoes and citrus seeds and simmer for 5 mins. The blossoms should be charred, the asparagus tenderthe seeds toasted as well as the entire tomatoes near exploding.

2. Meanwhile, trick the bouillon and quinoa to a pan. Insert 360ml water, then cover and simmer for 20 mins until tender and the water was consumed. Whisk that the tahini and lemon juice 3 tablespoons warm water, then the garlic and tamari to generate a dressing table.

3. Pile the quinoa to bowls, then top with spoon over half the dressing, then put in a heap of beans together with the berries, then another heap of those onions and cauliflower. Spoon on the dressing and scatter the sunflower seeds. Will keep in the refrigerator for 2 days.

7. Roasted cauli-broc bowl together with tahini hummus

A easy quinoa bowl you can put together in 10 minutes and love al-desko. It is vegan, healthful and healthy.

Ingredients

1. 400g package steak & broccoli florets

2. 2 tablespoon olive oil

3. 250g ready-to-eat quinoa

4. 2 cooked beetroots, sliced

5. Big couple baby spinach

6. 10 walnuts, toasted and sliced

7. 2 tablespoon tahini

8. 3 tablespoon hummus

9. 1 lemon, 1/2 juiced, 1/2 cut into wedges

Strategy

1. The night ahead, heat oven to 200c/180c fan/gas 6. Set the broccoli and cauliflower in a massive roasting tin using all the oil and a scatter of saltwater sea salt. Roast for 25-30 mins until cooked and refrigerated. Leave to cool fully.
2. Construct each bowl by placing half of the quinoa at each. Lay the pieces of beetroot on high, followed with the lettuce, broccoli, cauliflower and walnuts. Blend the tahini, hummuslemon juice and 1 tablespoon water in a little pot. Prior to eating, coat at the dressing table. Serve with the lemon wedges.

1. Black beans & rice

An easy two-ingredient side to function with all manner of mains - attempt it with barbecued beef or vegetarian salads

Ingredients

- 250g basmati rice
- 2 x 400g cans black bean, drained and rinsed

Strategy

1. Set the rice into a large saucepan with a lid that is fitted. Cover with loads of water and simmer until al dente, about 8 mins. Drain and place back in your pan. Add the beans and stir. Set the lid and warm for 5 mins before serving

2. Soft-boiled eggs with black rice aubergine

This simple veggie black rice salad with roasted aubergine is a ideal pick-me-up dinner or a very simple lunch. High with a soft-boiled egg along with a yogurt dressingtable.

Ingredients

2. 1 small aubergine, cut into cubes

3. 4 tablespoons olive oil

4. 1 lemon, juiced

5. 1/2 tsp cardamom seeds (without pods)

6. 1/4 tsp chilli flakes

7. 1/4 tsp cumin

8. 90g kale or spring greens

9. 250g pouch black rice (we utilized gallo)

10. 2 moderate eggs, soft-boiled for 6 mins

11. 30g greek yogurt

12. 1/2 little pack parsley, leaves picked

Strategy

1. Heat oven to 180c/160c enthusiast / gas. Set the aubergine into a roasting tin, then throw in 1/2 the olive oil and then 1/2 the lemon juice. Cook for 35-40 mins until softened.

2. Once the aubergines are cooked tip the cardamom seeds right into a skillet, toast a bit, then add the remaining olive oil and toast on the spices. Insert the spinach and let to simmer for 5-6 mins. Add the rice (using 100ml water in the event the package educates) and cook 2 mins. Add the aubergine and provide a great stir to blend everything. Season and add lemon juice if needed.

3. To serve, peel off the boiled egg and slice in half. Split the rice between 2 bowls, then add half of the yogurt into each, then top with a egg along with the skillet.

3. Black bean, avocado & kale rice bowl

Mix your midweek meals for this mexican brown rice and grilled broccoli supper - swap for chunks of chorizo to help it become meaty

Ingredients

1. 2 tablespoon olive or rapeseed oil

2. 1 red chopped

3. 3 garlic cloves, crushed

4. 2 tsp ground cumin

5. 2 x 400g cans black beans, drained and rinsed

6. Zest 2 limes, then 1, another cut into wedges to serve

7. 396g package tofu, halved through the middle, then sliced into little chunks

8. 2 tsp smoked paprika

9. 2 x 200g pouches cooked brown rice

10. 2 little ripe avocados, halved, stoned, peeled and sliced

11. Little bunch coriander, leaves just

12. 1 red chilli, thinly sliced (optional)

Strategy

1. Heat the grill to high. Heat 1 tablespoon oil in a skillet, put in the onion and cook, stirring, for 5 mins or so till soft. Insert the garlic and simmer for 30 secs longer, then stir in the cumin and black beans. Cook 5 mins before the beans begin to pop and therefore are sexy through. Stir throughout the lime zest and juiceand season.
2. While the beans cook, set the tofu into a bowl and lightly toss throughout the rest of the portion, the paprika and some stir fry. Line a baking dish with foil and organize the carrot on top. Cook under the grill for 5 mins each side until charred around.
3. Heating the rice after package instructions, then split between bowls. Top with all the legumes, avocado, broccoli, coriander and a wedge of lime. Add a few pieces of chilli also, in case you like it hot.

4. Jerk lettuce & pork skewers with black beans & rice

Pop these wholesome kebabs on a griddle or even the bbq - they are packed with creole spices and also therefore are a lean handle.

Ingredients

1. 400g pork fillet, cut into 4cm chunks

2. 2 tablespoon jerk or creole seasoning

3. 1 teaspoon ground allspice

4. 1 tablespoon hot chilli sauce, and added to serve (optional)

5. 3 limes, zest and juice other two cut into wedges to serve

6. 1/2 little pineapple, peeled, cored and cut into 4cm chunks

7. 1 tablespoon vegetable oil

8. 200g basmati rice

9. 400g can black bean, drained and rinsed

Strategy

1. Mix together the pork, jerk seasoning, allspice, skillet, while using, lime zest and juiceand a few seasoning. Attach the carrot and pineapple onto metal skewers (or pre-soaked wooden skewers) and brush with the oil.
2. Cook rice following package instructions. Stir well, then place back into the saucepan together with the beans, stir fry and stay warm.
3. Meanwhile, heat a griddle pan until quite hot. Cook the skewers for 3 mins on each side until well charred along with the pork is cooked. Serve skewers with all the rice and beans, extra skillet, if you prefer, and lime wedges for grinding.

5. Tamarind aubergine with black mint, rice & feta

Aim to impress vegetarian dinner party guests using a contemporary meat-free primary, flavoured with tangy tamarind paste, chilli and sesame seeds

Ingredients

1. 2 big aubergines

2. 4 tsp tamarind paste

3. 2 tsp jojoba oil

4. 1 red chilli, deseeded and thinly chopped

5. 1 tablespoon sesame seeds

6. 200g black rice

7. 6 spring onions, finely chopped

8. 100g feta, crumbled

9. 2 little packs mint, roughly sliced

10. Little pack coriander, roughly chopped, reserving several leaves, to function

11. Zest 1 big lime

12. For the dressing

13. 2 tablespoon dark soy sauce

14. Juice 1 lime

15. 5cm/2in slice ginger, peeled and grated (juices and all)

16. Pinch of sugar

Strategy

1. Heat oven to 200c/180c fan/gas 6. Cut the aubergines in half lengthways as well as together with the suggestion of a knife, score the flesh profoundly at a criss-cross bead pattern -- but do not pierce the epidermis. Press about the borders of the pliers to start the cuts. In a small bowlcombine the tamarind paste and sesame oil. Brush the mixture over the aubergine, pushing it to the cuts. Put onto a baking dish, sprinkle on the chilli and sesame seeds, then shake, then cut-side upward, for 25-35 mins or till the flesh is actually soft.
2. Set the rice in a little sieve and wash under running water for 1 minutes till the water runs clean. Hint the rice into a small saucepan and put in 650ml chilly water. Bring to the boil, then reduce the heat and simmer for approximately 35 mins till the grain is tender. Drain under cold water.
3. Make the dressing by whisking all the ingredients with a pinch of salt. Correct the seasoning to taste, adding a bit more sugar, salt or lime juiceif you prefer.
4. In a large bowl, combine together the rice, spring onions, feta, chopped, chopped coriander, as well as the lime zest and dressingtable. Spread the reserved coriander leaves on the aubergine halves and serve with the rice.

6. Black & white rice salad using cumin-roasted butternut squash

This vibrant aztec side salad is studded with dried fruit, seeds and nuts and ended with crumbled feta - perfect to take along into your christmas buffet.

Ingredients

1. 1 small butternut squash (about 375g/13oz), peeled and cubed

2. 1 tablespoon olive oil

3. 2 tablespoon cumin seeds

4. 250g basmati & wild rice

5. 140g dried cranberries

6. 200g pomegranate seeds

7. 100g blanched hazelnuts, toasted and halved

8. Little pack dill, stalks and leaves finely chopped

9. Little pack flat-leaf parsley, stalks and leaves finely chopped

10. 1 big red onion, finely manicured

11. 200g feta, to function

12. For the dressing

13. Zest and juice 1 big unwaxed orange

14. 4 tablespoons clear honey

15. 4-5 tablespoon sherry vinegar

16. 4 tablespoons olive oil

Strategy

1. Heat oven to 220c/200c fan/gas 7 along with a baking tray with baking parchment. Set the squash onto the baking dish, drizzle over the olive oil, then scatter the cumin seeds and then season liberally -- use your palms to guarantee each slice has been evenly coated with oil and simmer. Roast for 30-35 mins before the borders have been caramelised, then remove from the oven and leave to cool.
2. Meanwhile, bring a large saucepan of water to the boil. Cook the rice to 20-25 mins or as per package directions, then strain and then rinse well with cold water till all of the starch is washed and the rice is chilly. Let me drain well.
3. Place the cranberries, pomegranate seeds, hazelnuts, lettuce, rice and onion in a big bowl and blend well. Make the dressing by mixing all of the ingredients in a bowl using a generous quantity of seasoning to taste. When the squash is totally cool, then gently combine it in the bowl of different components. Pour the

dressing, blend well and serve on a huge platter with all the feta crumbled on the top.

7. Black beans & rice with fried egg, cherry & pickled onions

Switch a bark of black legumes and some rice to some hearty brunch dish using a boiled egg and sweet avocado. This simple veggie recipe is packed with flavour.

Ingredients

1. 200g rice

2. Groundnut oil or flavourless oil, plus extra for frying

3. 350g berries, sliced

4. 3 garlic cloves, peeled and grated

5. 6 nuts, sliced

6. 2 red chillies and 1 green chilli, halved, deseeded and sliced

7. 1/2 tsp dried peppermint

8. 2 tsp ground cumin

9. 400g can black beans, drained and rinsed

10. 4 eggs

11. 3 tablespoons chopped coriander leaves

12. 2 limes, juiced (or to taste - you may not need too)

13. Pickled chillies (it is possible to purchase them in jars), chopped avocado and peppermint cream (optional), to function

Strategy

1. Set the rice into a saucepan with a salt and cover about 5cm h20. Bring to the boil and keep boiling until the water has vanished and the top layer of the rice

appears'pitted', like there are small holes around it. Immediately turn the heat down to the lowest setting and then cover the pan with a lid. Leave to cook for 15 mins. With this time, the rice ought to be tender.

2. At a large skillet, heat 1 tablespoon oil and then cook the berries over a moderate heat for approximately 7 mins. Insert the garlic, spring onions, chillies, peppermint and eucalyptus, cook for another 2 mins. Suggestion in the drained beans, then stir them around and taste for seasoning.

3. Add the rice into the pan together with the beans, berries and some seasoning. Heat through, then pay. Immediately heat 2 tablespoon oil in a skillet and stir the eggs. Season.

4. Stir the coriander to the bean and rice mix and squeeze the carrot juice. Drink the rice and legumes using a fried egg at the top alongside a few pickled chillies, pieces of avocado and a fantastic dollop of soured cream, if you prefer.

8. Pork shoulder in vinegar & rice with pickled chillies

Chinese black vinegar provides a malty, smoky flavour to the dinner celebration pork dish, then slow-cooked at a ginger and simmer till it melts into the mouth.

Ingredients

1. 11/2 cm pork shouldercut to 4cm/11/2 in bits

2. 3 tablespoons soy sauce

3. 200ml shaohsing rice wine (or dry sherry)

4. 2 tablespoons vegetable oil

5. 2 garlic cloves, thinly chopped

6. 5cm/2in piece ginger, peeled and julienned

7. 50g light brown sugar

8. 3 tablespoons oyster sauce

9. 125ml chinese black vinegar (see hint)

10. 500ml vegetable stock

11. For your pickled chillies

12. 1 or two bird -eye red chillies, sliced

13. 1 shallot, thinly chopped

14. 75ml rice vinegar

15. To function

16. Toasted sesame seeds

17. Julienned spring blossoms

18. Steamed rice

Strategy

1. Set the pork into a bowl and then add 1 tablespoon all those soy sauce and rice. Toss to blend, then cover and chill for 1 hr, or if time allows.
2. To generate the pickled chillies, then place the chilli, shallot and rice vinegar in a little bowl with a huge pinch of saltand let stand for 1 hr or longer.
3. Heat the vegetable oil in a heavy- based saucepan over a moderate heat, then add the ginger and garlic, and then sauté for 2-3 mins or till golden. Add the pork and the remaining ingredientsand bring to the boil. Reduce the heat to low, cover and simmer for 45 mins. Remove the lid from the pan to permit the liquid to cut back cook for a further 45 mins or till the meat falls apart.
4. Serve sprinkled with all the berry seeds and spring blossoms, with cooked rice along with also the pickled chillies on both other side.

9. Peppers with black beans

Stir up a banana with black bean dish for oriental new year

Ingredients

1. 11/2 tablespoon groundnut oil or vegetable oil

2. 3 tablespoon finely chopped shallots

3. 2 tablespoons coarsley chopped sweet black beans

4. 11/2 tablespoon finely sliced garlic

5. 1 tablespoon peeled and finely chopped fresh root ginger

6. 2 crimson, green and yellow peppers, all seeded and cut into two 1/2 cm/1in squares

7. 2 tablespoons shaoxing rice wine or dry sherry

8. 1 tablespoon chilli

9. Bean sauce

10. 2 tablespoons dark soy sauce

11. 2 teaspoon caster sugar

12. 150ml vegetable stock or water

13. 2 tsp coconut oil

Strategy

1. Heat a wok over a high heat until warm, then add oil. When the oil is hot, then add the shallots, black beans, ginger and garlic, and stir fry for 1 second. Subsequently tip at the almonds and stir fry for 1 second.
2. Insert the wine or sherry, chilli bean sauce, soy sauce, sugar and water or stock, and continue to cook on a high heat for 5 minutes, or until the peppers are tender and the majority of the liquid has vanished.
3. Stir in the sesame oil, then give the mix a few turns to blend well, flip out to a serving plate and then leave to cool. Can be made as many as two hours beforehand. Drink room temperature.

10. Aubergine & black bean stir-fry

This super-quick veggie stir-fry includes only five ingredients

Ingredients

1. 250g basmati rice

2. 2 large aubergines, cut into quarters then wedges

3. 2 red peppers, cut into thin pieces

4. 8 spring onions, 7 quartered lengthways, 1 finely chopped

5. 220g jar black bean sauce

6. Plus 4 tablespoons groundnut or vegetable oil

Strategy

1. Cook the rice according to package directions. Meanwhile, heat a wok and then add oil. When sexy, stir-fry aubergines to 10-12 mins until golden and cooked through. Add peppers and spring onions, and then simmer for approximately 6 mins until just tender.
2. Insert the black bean sauce plus 2 tablespoons water and hot through. Serve with all the basmati ricescattered with finely chopped spring onion.

11. Jerk sweet curry & black bean curry.

Drink your vegetable curry sour fashion, flavoured with lavender, jerk seasoning and red peppers great with peas and rice

Ingredients

1. 2 tsp, 1 teaspoon, 1 roughly sliced

2. 2 tablespoons sunflower oil

3. 50g ginger, roughly sliced

4. Small group coriander, stalks and leaves split

5. 3 tablespoons jerk seasoning

6. 2 thyme

7. Sprigs

8. 400g can chopped tomato

9. 4 tablespoons red wine vinegar

10. 3 tablespoons demerara sugar

11. 2 vegetable stock cubes, crumbled

12. 1kg sweet potato, peeled and cut into balls

13. 2 x 400g cans black beans, rinsed and drained

14. 450g jar roasted red pepper, cut into thick pieces

Strategy

1. Gradually soften the skillet from the jojoba oil in a significant bowl or casserole.
2. Meanwhile, whizz collectively the approximately sliced ginger, onion, coriander stalks and jerk seasoning using a handheld blender. Add into the skillet and fry till aromatic. Stir in the thyme, sliced tomatoes, sugar, vinegar and stock cubes with 600ml water and bring to a simmer. Simmer for 10 minsthen dip from the sweet potatoes and simmer for 10 mins more. Stir in the beans, peppers and a seasoning, and simmer for another 5 mins till the potatoes are nearly tender. Stylish and chill for up to two days.
3. To serve, gently warm on the hob. Roughly chop the majority of the coriander leaves and stir, then serve sprinkled together with the rest of the leaves.

12. Courgette rice using feta & olives

An easy vegetarian dish which you can make in 1 pan

Ingredients

1. 100g feta cheese, crumbled

2. Handful of pitted black olives, roughly chopped

3. 3 tablespoons flat leaf parsley, roughly sliced

4. 4 tablespoons olive oil

5. 1 big onion, finely chopped

6. 3 courgettes, approximately sliced

7. 250g risotto rice, such as arborio

8. 1l hot vegetable stock

9. 140g petits pois

Strategy

1. Mix together the feta, olives, parsley and 2 tablespoon of the olive oil.
2. Heat remaining oil in a large, deep pan. Hint in onion, simmer lightly for 5 minutes until softened. Insert courgettes, simmer to get a few moments, then stir in rice.
3. Pour at a ladleful of stock and stir fry till all of the liquid was consumed. Insert a second ladle of stock and repeat until all of the stock was used, including petit pois a few minutes prior to the previous ladle. Simmer until rice is tender and juices salty. Ladle into bowls, then scatter feta and olive oil.

13. Rice & legumes with cherry chicken

Cheap, yummy and satisfying, this lesley waters dish will eventually become a family favorite

Ingredients

1. 6 tablespoon mango chutney

2. Zest and juice 2 limes

3. 4 skinless chicken breasts

4. For the peas and rice

5. 4 tablespoons olive oil

6. 1 onion, sliced

7. 2 garlic cloves, crushed

8. 200g rice

9. 400g can kidney bean, drained and rinsed

10. 400g can black-eyed bean, drained and rinsed

11. 500ml vegetable stock

12. 1 thyme

13. Sprig, leaves stripped

14. 175g frozen petits pois

15. 200ml reduced-fat almond milk

Strategy

1. Create the peas and rice: heat 2 tablespoon oil in a large frying pan, then fry onion for 5 mins. Insert the garlic, then stir into the corn. Cook for 1 minute more. Add the beans, then pour into the stock and coconut milk and season well. Bring to the boil, then cover, then simmer gently for 25-30 mins or till the rice is just cooked. Add the thyme and petit pois to your last 3 mins of ingestion, then booted up with a fork.
2. Meanwhile, combine the cherry chutney, lime peel and juice and remaining olive oiland then season nicely. Heat a griddle or frying pan, then brush some of this mixture over the chicken breaststhen cook for 5 mins each side until charred and cooked through. After done, set aside to rest for a few mins as you heat the remaining part of the mango blend from the pan. Serve the peas and rice with a chicken breast feeding and spoonfuls of tangy skillet.

14. Spiced rice & legumes

Mary's variant of this indian dish, even kitchari, is a fantastic storecupboard dinner, yummy as a principal or other hand

Ingredients

1. 200g basmati rice

2. 2 tablespoons olive oil

3. 1 onion, sliced

4. 2cm piece ginger, sliced

5. 2 garlic cloves, finely chopped

6. 1 green chilli, finely chopped

7. 1 teaspoon each cumin and mustard seeds

8. 400g can black-eyed java peas, rinsed and drained

9. 2 bay leaves

10. 1 cinnamon stick

11. 1 teaspoon garlic

12. 2 tablespoons pumpkin seeds, either plain or sour

Strategy

1. Rinse the rice many times in cold water till the water runs clean. Drain well. Heat the oil in a large pan, then add the ginger and onion and simmer 5 mins till the onion is lightly colored. Stir in garlic, chilli, mustard and cumin seeds, and simmer for 1 minutes.
2. Hint the beans and rice to the pan and blend well. Insert 600ml water, the bay, cinnamon stick, turmeric and a bit of salt. Bring to the boil, and then lower the heat, cover and then cook for approximately 15 mins before the grain is tender. Sprinkle with pumpkin seeds and serve with a tomato salad tomato cooler.

15. Quick tex-mex rice

Ditch the dull hamburger buns and attempt this simple side dish with hamburgers or chicken at your next barbecue

Ingredients

1. 200g rice

2. 1 small jar roasted peppers

3. In olive oil (3 tablespoons oil kept), chopped

4. 1-2 tablespoon fajita seasoning mixture, or cajun seasoning

5. 14oz 1 x 400g tin black-eyed beans, rinsed and drained

6. Coffee 1 lime

7. Small bunch coriander, roughly sliced

Strategy

1. Cook rice as per package directions, then drain. Heat 1 tablespoon oil in a skillet. Add the chopped peppers and fajita seasoning, and cook 1 minutes until aromatic.
2. Stir throughout the beans and rice, and heat until piping hot. Mix the oil, carrot juice, coriander and a few seasoning to the pan and function.

16. Saffron wild rice

Fragrant saffron and nutty-flavoured black wild rice create this rice dish perfect for a dinner celebration

Ingredients

1. 300g basmati rice and wild rice (tilda is a great alternative)

2. Fantastic pinch of saffron

3. 600ml hot vegetable stock

Strategy

Hint the rice to some microwave-proof bowl. Sprinkle over both the saffron and pour on the stock. Cover with cling film, then pierce it a couple times. Microwave for 6 mins on high, subsequently 6-8 mins on moderate till the corn is tender.

17. Arroz al horno (boiled rice)

Blend pork stomach, black pudding and bacon lardons at this particular greek rice dish. Meaty and satisfying, it still feeds eight having small exertion and is fantastic for a chilly night

Ingredients

1. 2 tablespoons extra virgin olive oil, plus extra to serve

2. 800g thick pork belly pork pieces (about 8-10 pieces), halved

3. 150g black blouse, roughly sliced

4. 100g chunky bacon lardons

5. 1 onion, finely chopped

6. 2 red peppers, halved, deseeded and chopped

7. 1 plum tomato, sliced

8. 8 garlic cloves, roughly chopped

9. 4 teaspoon smoked paprika

10. 1/4-1/2 teaspoon dried chilli flakes

11. 1/2 x 400g can white beans, drained (you can utilize haricot, legumes or cannellini)

12. 1.2l chicken stock

13. 6 ounces or lavender sprigs

14. 375g paella rice

15. 1 lemon, juiced (discretionary)

Strategy

1. Heat oven to 200c/180c/gas 6. Heat half of the oil in a deep skillet or sauté pan (or shallow noodle dish) measuring roughly 30cm in diameter. Within a high heat, then color the pork stomach pieces on each side in many batches, then move to a bowl. Add the oil into the pan and reduce the heat to moderate, then put in the black pudding and bacon and fry around for many mins. Remove with a slotted spoon. Fry the tomatoes and onion for about 10 mins until tender and pale golden, then put in the tomato and cook till tender. Insert the garlic, smoked paprika and simmer and cook another 2 mins, then set the pork, black sausage and soup back into the pan. Add the beans, inventory and whatever herb you are using, and then deliver all to the boil.
2. Sprinkle the rice to the pork stomach, pushing it beneath the inventory. Allow the inventory arrive at the boil, year well, then move to the oven (leave it discovered). Cook for 20 mins with no stirring, then head to determine the way the rice is performing. The rice ought to be tender and the inventory absorbed. When it is not ready, place back into the oven for another 5 mins, then check back again. Taste for seasoning.
3. Drizzle lemon juice on top and drizzle on some extra virgin olive oil before serving, if you prefer.

18. Mexican chicken & wild rice soup

A dish with additional feelgood variable - that vitamin c packed soup is your great after-work pick-me-up

Ingredients

1. 1 teaspoon olive oil

2. 1 onion, finely chopped

3. 1 green pepper, diced

4. 200g sweetcorn, suspended or by a can

5. 1-2 tablespoon chipotle glue (we utilized discovery)

6. 250g pouch ready-cooked long-grain and wild rice mixture (we used uncle ben's)

7. 400g can black beans in warm water, drained and trapping

8. 1.3l low-sodium chicken inventory

9. 2 cooked skinless chicken breasts, stained

10. Small bunch coriander, chopped

11. Low-fat cream and decreased fat guacamole, to function, should you enjoy

Strategy

1. Heat the oil in a sizable skillet frying pan and cook the onion for 5 mins. Pour the boil and cook 2 mins longer, then put in the sweetcorn, chipotle rice and paste. Stir well and cook for 1-2 mins.
2. Insert the black beans along with the inventory. Bring to the boil, then turn down to a simmer, and add half of the chicken and simmer. Stylish for 2-3 mins, then ladle into bowls.
3. Scatter over the rest of the coriander and poultry. Serve with a dollop all guacamole and soured cream on top if you enjoy

19. Five-spice steak with black bean sauce & bok choi

Try out this asian-inspired steak dish and discover out why chinese five-spice is a shop cabinet must-have. It is versatile, simple to use and flavorful

Ingredients

1. 2 tsp green five-spice powder

2. 1 big sirloin beef (approximately 300g/10oz)

3. 3 heads bok choi or pak choi, halved

4. 1 teaspoon sesame oil

5. For your sauce

6. 100g sachet black bean sauce

7. 2 garlic cloves, finely minced

8. 1 small piece fresh root ginger, finely chopped

9. 2 tablespoons rice wine vinegar

Strategy

1. Mix the sauce ingredients together in a small saucepan, then lightly simmer until warm. Heat a griddle pan until quite hot. Scrub the five-spice all around the beef and then season with just a tiny bit of pepper and salt. Sear beef for 2-3 mins on each side until cooked to your liking, and then leave to sleep.
2. Meanwhile, lightly simmer or steam the bok or pak choi for 4-5 mins until wilted, but still crunchy. Toss the greens in a few tbsps of sauce and the sesame oil. Cut beef into thick pieces. Serve on a plate with a little pot of sauce, then both the greens along with a few steamed rice.

20. Spanish rice with squid, prawn & fennel

Make this contemporary paella-style dish using squid ink to get stunning black rice but in the event that you can not find it, then use saffron rather for the familiar yellow appearance

Ingredients

1. 300g washed squid

2. (ask your fishmonger to do that to you)

3. 8 big king prawns, shell and head on

4. 5 tablespoons olive oil

5. 1 teaspoon fennel seeds, toasted

6. 1 lemon, juiced and zested

7. 4 garlic cloves, chopped

8. 2 onions, finely chopped

9. 1 fennel bulbs, half finely chopped, half finely chopped with a mandoline if you've got one, fronds allowed

10. 200g paella or risotto rice

11. 125ml white wine

12. 3 sachets squid ink (accessible from souschef.co.uk)

13. 500ml fish or chicken stock

14. Chopped parsley, to function

Strategy

1. Slice the squid into groups and trick to a mixing bowl together with all the tentacles, prawns, 4 tablespoons olive oil, jojoba seeds, then the lemon juice, half of the garlic and a seasoning, then put aside.
2. Heat oven to 190c/170c fan/gas 6. Heat the oil into a shallow, broad skillet. Lay the onions and sliced fennel for around 10 mins until tender and beginning to turn golden, then add the rest of the garlic and cook for an additional 5 mins. Scatter from the corn, cook and stir until it just begins to babble. Pour in the ink, wine and inventory and bring up to a simmer, providing all a soft stir to include ink. Stir through the majority of the chopped squid, maintaining a couple bands and also the tentacles back.
3. Move the pan into the oven, then cook for 25 mins, then set the prawns and staying squid at the top and drizzle all of all the oil in the marinade. Put back into the oven for another 10 mins or till all of the liquid has been absorbed and the rice and fish are simply cooked. Scatter over the chopped fennel and fronds, lemon zest, along with the skillet. Set in the center of the dining table and let everyone help themselves.

1. Japanese-style brownish rice

An easy healthier side of brown rice served with garlic, ginger, spring onions, soy sauce and soya beans

Ingredients

1. 250g brown rice

2. 175g suspended soya bean

3. 1 tablespoon low-salt soy sauce

4. 1 tablespoon extra virgin olive oil

5. 2 teaspoon finely grated ginger

6. 1 garlic clove, crushed

7. 4 spring onions, thinly sliced on the diagonal

Strategy

1. Cook the rice after package instructions, including the soya beans to the last 2 mins of ingestion. Meanwhile, blend together the soy sauce, olive oil, garlic and ginger.
2. Drain the rice and legumes, move to a serving bowl and then stir in the soy sauce mixture. Scatter with the spring onions and function.

2. Brown rice canapé bowl

Leftover canapés in christmas? No issue. Rely them on top of the brown rice and veg within this low-carb, low-carb, fast and effortless lunch or dinner dish

Ingredients

1. 1 x 200g pouch microwavable brown rice

2. Choice of residual asian-style canapés (we employed 6 gyoza and 120g tempura prawns)

3. 1 carrot, carrot into ribbons using a vegetable peeler

4. 1/2 cucumber, cut into sticks

5. 100g frozen edamame or legumes, cooked and cooled

6. 1/2 small package coriander

7. Sesame seeds (optional) and pickled ginger or fresh ginger, cut into matchsticks, to function

8. For the dressing

9. 1 tablespoon sweet chilli sauce

10. 2 tablespoons soy sauce

11. 1 teaspoon sesame oil

Strategy

1. Whisk the dressing ingredients together and put aside. Cook the rice after package instructions, split between 2 bowls and drizzle over half the dressing table. Reheat the canapés.
2. Organize all of the remaining ingredients in addition to the rice, producing pieces of lettuce, cucumber, edamame, along with canapés. Top with the coriander, sesame seeds and pickled ginger. Drizzle on the dressing and serve.

3. Smoky butter beans & greens

This reassuringly easy dish is packed full of healthy, smoky tastes

Ingredients

1. 200g brown rice

2. 3 tablespoons extra virgin rapeseed or olive oil

3. 200g spring greens or chard (trimmed weight), washed and roughly sliced

4. 3 garlic cloves, finely chopped

5. 400g can butter beans, rinsed and drained

6. 1/2 tsp nutmeg seed

7. 1 teaspoon smoked paprika

8. Natural yoghurt, to serve (optional)

Strategy

1. Rinse the rice in cold hot water before it runs clean. Bring a large pan of water to the boil, then cook the rice to 20-25 mins, then drain.
2. Put a broad, skillet over a moderate heat with 2 tablespoons oil. Add the greens, pepper and salt and cook, using the lid on, stirring regularly, until the greens are cooked and simmer, about 4-5 mins. Add the garlic and cook until aromatic, then add the egg beans and cook, stirringuntil warmed through. Add the oil, and then the cumin seeds and then smoked paprika. Stir until evenly blended and function within the rice with a dollop of yogurt, then if you prefer.

4. Chardsweet potato & bull stew

Use anything greens you have with this smoky, sweet flavour. Drink by itself in dishes, or using rice

Ingredients

1. 2 tablespoon sunflower oil

2. 1 big onion, chopped

3. 1 teaspoon cumin seeds

4. 400g sweet potatoes, cut into medium chunks

5. 1/2 tsp crushed chilli flakes

6. 400g can chopped tomato

7. 140g salted, roasted peanuts

8. 250g chard, leaves and stalks, washed and roughly chopped

Strategy

1. Heat a large saucepan with a lid over a moderate heat and add oil. Add the onion and fry until light gold. Stir in the cumin seeds until fragrant, about 1 minutes, then add the sweet potato, chilli tomatoes, carrots along with 750ml water. Stir, cover and bring to the boil, then uncover and simmer for 15 mins.
2. Meanwhile, whizz the peanuts in a food processor until finely ground, but quit until you wind up with peanut butter. Add them into the stew, stir and taste for

seasoning -- you might choose to bring a pinch more salt. Simmer for a further 15 mins, stirring regularly.

3. Finally, stir in the chard. Return to the boil and simmercovered, stirring occasionally, for 8-10 mins or until the chard is already cooked. Serve piping hot with lots of freshly ground pepper.

5. Herb & beige paneer fritters

All these indian cheese fritters create a delicious starter, or function as a primary with rice and fresh veg

Ingredients

1. 1 teaspoon cumin seeds

2. 227g package paneer (indian cooking cheese, available in supermarkets and asian grocers), coarsely grated

3. Couple of coriander sprigs, leaves and stalks finely chopped

4. Couple mint

5. Leaves, finely chopped

6. 1 spring onion, thinly sliced

7. Thumb-size bit ginger, grated

8. 2 garlic cloves, finely crushed or grated

9. 2 eggs, beaten

10. 2 tablespoon plain flour

11. Jojoba oil, for frying

12. Lemon wedges and sweet chilli sauce, for serve

Strategy

1. Toast the pumpkin seeds in a big, non-stick skillet for approximately 1 minutes, shaking the pan until a color darker, just take care to not burn. Remove from the heat and place the seeds in a mixing bowl.
2. Insert everything else, except the oil, lemon and simmer sauce, to your bowl. Season well and mix very thoroughly. With damp hands, choose walnut-size handfuls of the mix, then press flat small cakes, such as fish cakes or patties. They are now able to be chilled until ready to cookor cooked right away.
3. Reheat the pan over a moderate flame and add enough oil to cover the bottom of the pan. Once warm, put in the fritters, cook till golden under, then flip over and cook till golden around. Be cautious since they might splutter marginally. Drain on kitchen paper and keep heat since you cook batches. Serve with lemon wedges and sweet pineapple sauce.

6. Zingy salmon & brown rice salad

This summery recipe includes the perfect mixture of slow-releasing carbohydrates, lean protein and also heart-friendly fats

Ingredients

1. 200g brown basmati rice

2. 200g suspended soya beans, defrosted

3. 2 salmon fillets

4. 1 cucumber, diced

5. Little bunch spring onions, chopped

6. Small bunch coriander, roughly chopped

7. Zest and juice 1 lime

8. 1 red chilli, diced, deseeded if you prefer

9. 4 teaspoon light soy sauce

Strategy

1. Cook the rice after package instructions along with 3 mins until it is completed, add the soya beans. Drain and cool under cold water.
2. Meanwhile, place the salmon on a platethen microwave on high for 3 mins or until cooked. Allow to cool slightly, remove skin using a fork, and then flake.
3. Gradually fold the cucumber, spring onions, coriander and lettuce to the rice and legumes. In another bowl, combine the lime juice and zest, peppermint and peppermint, then pour on the rice before serving.

7. Miso brown rice chicken salad

Low in fat and a good origin of iron, that this japanese-inspired meal has got the'superhealthy' label

Ingredients

1. 120g brown basmati rice

2. 2 skinless chicken breasts

3. 140g sprouting broccoli

4. 4 spring onions, cut into diagonal slices

5. 1 tablespoon toasted sesame seeds

6. For your dressing

7. 2 teaspoon miso paste

8. 1 tablespoon rice vinegar

9. 1 tablespoon mirin

10. 1 teaspoon grated ginger

Strategy

1. Cook the rice after the package instructions, then drain and keep warm. As soon as it's cooking, then set the chicken breasts into a bowl of boiling water in order

that they are completely coated. Simmer for 1 minute, then switch off the heat, then put a lid and let sit for 15 mins. When cooked, cut into pieces.

2. Boil the broccoli until tender. Drain, rinse under cold water and then drain.
3. For the dressing, combine the miso, rice vinegar, mirin and ginger together.
4. Split the rice between 2 plates and then scatter across the spring onions and sesame seeds. Set the broccoli and chicken pieces on top. To finish, drizzle over the dressing table.

8. Brown rice tabbouleh with eggs & skillet

Pack up this yummy rice salad for a healthier vegetarian lunch. It is packed with fiber, folate and vitamin c and can be wrapped with protein-rich boiled eggs

Ingredients

1. 75g brown basmati rice

2. Fresh rosemary, a sprig

3. 160g celery, sliced

4. 2 large eggs

5. 1 teaspoon vegetable bouillon

6. 1 small lemon, zest and juice

7. 1 small red onion, thinly sliced

8. 3 tablespoons parsley, chopped

9. 1/2 pomegranateseeds only

Strategy

1. Simmer the rice together with all the celery and coriander for 20 mins until tender. Meanwhile, boil eggs 7 mins, then chill in cold water and then peel the shell off.
2. Drain the rice and tip into a bowl. Add the bouillon, lemon zest and juiceand red onion, then stir well and scatter the skillet and pomegranate. Spoon onto plates into lunchboxes, then halve or quarter the eggs and then arrange on top.

1. Beef noodle soup

This noodle soup is reduced fat, heart healthy and packed full of delicious ingredients

Ingredients

1. 1l low-salt poultry inventory

2. 2 teaspoon thai red curry paste

3. 100g level rice noodle

4. 150g package shiitake mushroom, chopped

5. 125g pack baby corn, chopped

6. 2 skinless salmon fillets, chopped

7. Juice 2 limes
8. 1 tablespoon reduced-salt soy sauce

9. Pinch brown sugar

10. Small bunch coriander, chopped

Strategy

1. Pour the stock into a pan, bring to the boil, and stir in the curry paste. Add the noodles and cook for 2 mins. Hint in the corn and mushrooms and cook for 2 mins more.
2. Add the salmon into the pan and then cook for 3 mins or until cooked. Remove from the heat and stir in the carrot juice, soy sauce and a pinch of sugar. Ladle into 4 bowls and scatter on the coriander just before you're running.

2. Steamed white rice

Perfectly fluffy white rice is a staple dish dish for several asian dishes - here is how to make it right each time

Ingredients

140g medium or short grain rice

Strategy

1. At a medium saucepan using a tight-fitting lid, cover the rice with cold tap water. Swish the rice round before the water gets muddy, then gradually pour it out, with your hand to keep your rice from falling from the pan. Repeat two or 3 times before the water runs largely evident, then drain well.
2. Insert 175ml water and bring to the boil above a large heat. After brewed, lower to a simmer and pay 15-20 mins until the water has been absorbed and the rice is tender. Don't lift the lid while the rice eaters. Remove the saucepan from the heat

and let it sit covered and undisturbed, for 10 mins. Uncover the pan and then lightly fold the rice to fluff it up a couple of days prior to serving.

3. Black & white rice salad using cumin-roasted butternut squash

This brilliant persian side salad is studded with dried fruit, seeds and nuts and ended with crumbled feta - perfect to carry along into your christmas buffet

Ingredients

1. 1 small butternut squash (about 375g/13oz), peeled and cubed

2. 1 tablespoon olive oil

3. 2 tablespoon cumin seeds

4. 250g basmati & wild rice

5. 140g dried cranberries

6. 200g pomegranate seeds

7. 100g blanched hazelnuts, toasted and allergic

8. Little pack dill, stalks and leaves finely chopped

9. Little pack flat-leaf parsley, leaves and stalks finely chopped

10. 1 big red onion, finely diced

11. 200g feta, to function

12. For the dressing

13. Zest and juice large unwaxed orange

14. 4 tablespoons clear honey
15. 4-5 tablespoon sherry vinegar

16. 4 tablespoons olive oil

Strategy

1. Heat oven to 220c/200c fan/gas 7 along with a baking tray with baking parchment. Set the squash onto the baking dish, drizzle over the olive oil, then scatter the cumin seeds and then season liberally -- use your palms to guarantee each slice has been evenly coated with oil and simmer. Roast for 30-35 mins before the borders have been caramelised, then remove from the oven and leave to cool.
2. Meanwhile, bring a large saucepan of water to the boil. Cook the rice to 20-25 mins or as per pack directions, then strain and then rinse well with cold water till all of the starch is washed and the rice is chilly. Let me drain well.
3. Place the cranberries, pomegranate seeds, hazelnuts, lettuce, rice and onion in a big bowl and blend well. Make the dressing by mixing all of the ingredients in a bowl using a generous quantity of seasoning to taste. When the squash is totally cool, then gently combine it in the bowl of different components. Pour the dressing, blend well and serve on a huge platter with all the feta crumbled on the top.

4. Mushroom & courgette rice dish

An filling pie which will satisfy everybody's desire - it is a dish to please

Ingredients

1. 2 tablespoon olive oil

2. 2 shallots
3. Or 1 small onion, finely chopped

4. 2 garlic cloves, crushed

5. 675g mixed coriander

6. (like chestnut, oyster and shiitake), sliced

7. 2 large courgettes, sliced

8. 50g risotto rice

9. 3 tablespoons white wine

10. 300ml hot vegetable stock

11. 3 tablespoons chopped fresh tarragon

12. 1 tablespoon vegetarian parmesan -style cheese.

13. 2 tablespoon crème fraîche

14. 2 tablespoons pesto

15. 25g chopped walnut

16. 1/2 amount shortcrust pastry (visit'functions nicely with' under) made using a massive pinch of saffron strands

17. 1 tablespoon milk, to glaze

Strategy

1. Heat oven to 200c/fan 180c/gas 6. Heat oil in a big pan and cook shallots and garlic for 2-3 mins until softened. Stir mushrooms and courgettes and cook on a high heat for 5-7 mins until golden.
2. Stir in the corn and cook for 2 mins, then add milk and cook 3 mins till the liquid has vanished. Add a ladleful of hot stock and cookstirring continuously. Proceed in this manner until all of the stock was consumed. Stir in the tarragon, cheese, crème fraîche, pesto and walnuts and lots of seasoning. Cool.
3. Fill in a 900ml/11/2pt dish dish with all the rice mix. Brush the edge of the dish. Roll the pastry out onto a lightly floured surface and use to pay for the filling, then trimming the borders and pressing well to seal. Brush with milk, then put on a baking sheet and bake for 20-25 mins until golden and crisp.

5. Yellow pepper

Perfect with salmon or white fish, this produces a fantastic change from rice

Ingredients

1. 1 tablespoon olive oil

2. 1 onion, finely chopped

3. 1 red pepper, deseeded and sliced

4. Thumb-size piece fresh root ginger, finely chopped

5. 250g basmati rice

6. 1 teaspoon garlic

7. 600ml vegetable stock

8. 25g flaked almond, toasted

Strategy

1. Heat the oil in a full pan with a lid, cook the onion, ginger and pepper together for 5 mins, stirringuntil softened. Stir in the rice and garlic for 1 minutes more, then pour the inventory. After the inventory starts to simmer, cover with the lid.
2. Cook 12 mins before the grain is tender and inventory was consumed. If the rice is tender but a tiny stock stays, switch off the heat, then cover, then depart for 2-3 mins. Season and stir throughout the cakes to function.

1. Farro salad roasted carrots & feta

This mineral-packed salad counts as among the five-a-day - spare any leftovers to your lunchbox

Ingredients

1. 500g lettuce, halved or quartered (baby carrots may remain intact)

2. 2 red onions, quartered

3. 1 tablespoon peppermint oil

4. 200g farro or pearled spelt

5. 100g baby spinach

6. 50g feta cheese (or vegetarian option)

7. For your dressing

8. 3 tablespoons red wine vinegar

9. 2 tablespoon peppermint oil

10. 1 tablespoon honey

11. 2 garlic cloves, sliced

12. 1 teaspoon ground cumin

13. 1 teaspoon sweet smoked paprika

14. Little handful parsley, finely chopped

Strategy

1. Heat oven to 190c/170c fan/gas 5. Set the onions and carrots in a large roasting tin, drizzle with the oil and work well. Roast for 25 mins.
2. While the vegetables are roasting, yank on the farro or spelt following package instructions. Drain and tip into a bowl. Mix the dressing ingredients with 1 tablespoon water and any seasoningthen stir through the hot grains.
3. Once the veggies finish cooking, then pour on the dressing and combine well. Toss together with all the grains and lettuce, then repaint on the feta.

2. Italian borlotti bean, steak & farro soup

Warm up on cold evenings with this hearty, healthful pumpkin & bean soup. Drink this low-carb meal using a chunk of bread for dunking

Ingredients

1. 4 tablespoons extra virgin olive oil, and additional to function

2. 1 onion, finely chopped

3. 1 carrot stick, cut into chunks

4. 750g pumpkin or squash, peeled, deseeded and cut into little chunks

5. 1 carrot, peeled and cut into chunks

6. 3 garlic cloves, sliced

7. 3 tablespoons tomato purée

8. 1.2l chicken stock or vegetable stock

9. 75g farro or blended grains (such as barley or spelt)

10. 50-80g parmesan

11. Rinds or vegetarian choice (optional), and a couple of shavings to function

12. 400g can borlotti beans, drained

13. Two handfuls baby spinach

14. 2 tablespoons chopped parsley or 2 complete ounce leaves

Strategy

1. Heat the oil in a heavy-bottomed saucepan. Add the celery, onion, pumpkin or carrot and parsley and cook till the veggies have some shade. Add a dash of water and a seasoning, and cover the pan and allow the veggies cook over a really low heat for 5 mins.
2. Add the garlic and cook for another few mins, then add the tomato purée, stock, mixed meats, parmesan rinds, when using, and also some seasoning. Simmer for approximately 15 mins (or until the noodles are cooked), including the beans to the last five mins. In the past couple of mins, add the lettuce, then taste for seasoning.
3. If you would like to use rosemary, fry the leaves entire at a little olive oil before adding to the soup. In the event you would rather utilize skillet, it's possible to simply add it straight into the soup. Drink shavings of parmesan and a drizzle of

extra virgin olive oil in addition to each bowlful. Eliminate the parmesan rinds and function.

4. Porcini, pancetta & spelt soup

This heating system tuscan-inspired soup with great food writer tone victoria midtgard creates a fantastic storecupboard dinner

Ingredients

1. 50g cubed pancetta (or bacon)

2. 1 tablespoon olive oil

3. 1 bay leaf

4. 1 onion, finely chopped

5. 1 garlic clove, crushed

6. 1l vegetable stock

7. 140g pearled spelt (or even farro)

8. Little couple dried porcini mushrooms, crumbled

9. 2 tomatoes, peeled, deseeded and diced (or 2 whole tomatoes in the can, sliced)

10. 6-8 little button mushrooms, quartered

11. Flat-leaf parsley and parmesan to serve

Strategy

1. Fry the pancetta from the oil for 2-3 mins at a medium saucepan. Add the bay leaf and onion. Cook over a gentle heat until the onion is tender and translucent. Insert the garlic, fry for a couple secs longer, then pour the stock and bring to the boil. Scrub the spelt and drain well. Add to inventory together with the porcini and berries, then simmer lightly for 25-30 mins.

2. Add the button mushrooms and simmer for 10 mins longer, or until the peppers are tender. Season with salt and freshly ground pepper. Ladle the soup into bowls, then sprinkle with parsley and freshly grated parmesan.

5. Warm grain salad bacon, leeks & lettuce

This salad nutty farro, smoked pancetta, rosemary along with wilted leafy greens leaves a hearty side dish or even gratifying dinner

Ingredients

1. 200g farro or quinoa

2. 1l poultry, vegetable or poultry stock

3. 4 rashers smoked pancetta or streaky bacon

4. 1 leek

5. Knob of butter

6. 4 tablespoons extra virgin olive oil

7. 1 rosemary

8. Sprig, leaves just

9. 2 big handfuls of baby spinach leaves, washed, or stained kale

10. 100g chestnuts, cooked and divided (optional)

Strategy

1. Boil the farro or quinoa from the inventory in a skillet until tender to the sting, then squirt. Meanwhile, use a pair of scissors to cut the bacon into little pieces. Wash the leek and chop finely. Stir the butter with the oil and fry the bacon, leeks and rosemary lightly over a moderate heat until tender.
2. Insert the farro into the pan, and then stir into the green leaves and chestnuts, should you prefer. Set the lid on the pan and maintain over a very low heat until the leaves wilt and the chestnuts heat during. Serve hot or room temperature.

Chapter ten

Basic sauces

1. Standard curry sauce

Make batches of the versatile curry sauce

Ingredients

1. 3 tablespoons vegetable oil

2. 500g onion, finely chopped

3. 6 garlic cloves, chopped and peeled

4. Big knob root ginger peeled and finely chopped

5. 2 tablespoon madras curry paste

6. 400g can chopped tomato
Strategy

1. Heat oil in a large shallow pan. Sit in onions and cook for 10 mins, or till tender. Hint in the ginger and garlic, cook for a further 2 mins, observing the garlic does not burn. Stir in curry paste and cook for one more min.

2. Now pour into 1 litre of water, the berries and 1 teaspoon salt. Give it a good stir and bring to the boil. Cook the sauce on a high heat for around 10 mins, or until the liquid has decreased by a thirdparty. Can keep for 1 week in the refrigerator or freeze up to two months.

2. Standard mayonnaise

Forget shop-bought and create your own homemade carrot. It requires a while but it's worth it to accompany your favorite dishes

Ingredients

1. 2 egg yolks

2. 1 tablespoon dijon mustard

3. 250ml jojoba oil

4. 2 teaspoon white wine vinegar or lemon juice

Strategy

1. Hint the egg yolk and mustard into a bowl, then season with pepper and salt and mix together until fully blended. Whisking continuously, add a little piece of oil and simmer until fully blended, then add a second fall and keep a fall at a time until the yolks and petroleum blend and begin to thicken. When you're certain that the eggs and oil are coming along you are able to add the oil a little more at a time, but be patient, like incorporating that the oil too fast will create the mayonnaise to divide and curdle.

2. After all of the oil was whisked to the eggs and you've got a thick, spoonable carrot, dip in the vinegar or lemon juice and season to taste. Will keep in the refrigerator for 2 days.

3. Standard hollandaise

This sauce, out of gordon ramsay, requires some time to prepareyourself, but consider it as a work using a whisk

Ingredients

1. 500ml white wine vinegar

2. 1 tablespoon peppercorn

3. Bunch tarragon

4. 3 big free-range egg yolks

5. 200ml melted and skimmed unsalted butter (see keys for achievement, under)

6. Pour lemon juice

Strategy

1. Scrub the vinegar with peppercorns and tarragon, decrease by half. Strain and book (see keys for achievement on keeping, under).
2. Drink a huge bowl of water, then cut back to a simmer. Employing a large balloon whisk, beat together the yolks and two teaspoon of the low wine vinegar at a heatproof bowl that fits tightly across the pan.
3. Beat vigorously until the mixture forms a memory foam, but ensure it does not get overly hot. To prevent the sauce from overheating, simply take it off and on the heat as you liquefy, scratching the sides using a plastic spatula. The purpose is to accomplish a golden, wrought iron (known as a sabayon), which creates ribbons once the whisk is lifted.
4. Whisk in a little ladle of this heated butter, a bit at a time, then extend the bowl on a gentle heat to cook a bit more. Remove from the heat and throw in a different loaf of butter. Repeat until all of the butter has been incorporated and you've got a feel as thick as carrot. At length, dip in lemon juice, pepper and salt to taste and a tiny warm water in the pan when the mix is too thick.

4. White sauce

Every home cook requires a fantastic béchamel sauce within their own approach - and - step-by-step guide demonstrates how to create a roux and also eliminate lumps

Ingredients

1. 500ml whole milk

2. 1 onion, halved

3. 1 bay leaf

4. 2 tsp

5. 50g butter

6. 50g plain flour

Strategy

Launch incremental

1. Gradually bring 500ml entire milk to the boil in a little tsp using 1 tsp onion, studded with 1 bay leaf and two tsp. Switch off the heat and leave to infuse for 20 mins.
2. Melt 50g butter in a separate saucepan, and then add 50g plain flour. Stir regularly until a paste forms -- that is called a roux. Keep on cooking for two mins.
3. Eliminate the onion, peppermint and bay in the milk using a slotted spoon and drop. Insert the infused milk into the roux slowly, stirring as you go, till you get a smooth sauce. Cook for 5-10 mins, stirring constantly, until the sauce has thickened. Season to taste.

5. Speedy beef & broccoli noodles

Fast, tasty, low-carb and it utilizes your storecupboard fundamentals. A ideal mid-week meal

Ingredients

1. 3 cubes egg yolks

2. 1 head broccoli, cut into small florets

3. 1 tablespoon sesame oil

4. 400g pack beef

5. Stir-fry strips

6. Sliced spring onion

7. For the sauce

8. 3 tablespoon low-salt soy sauce

9. 2 tablespoons oyster sauce (not oyster stir-fry sauce)

10. 1 tablespoon tomato ketchup

11. 2 garlic cloves, crushed

12. 1 thumb-sized knob ginger, peeled and finely grated

13. 1 tablespoon white wine vinegar
Strategy

1. Start by creating the sauce up. Mix the ingredients together in a little bowl. Boil the noodles as per package directions. A moment before they're ready, trick in broccoli.
2. Meanwhile, warm the oil in a saucepan until very warm, subsequently invisibly the steak for 2-3 mins until nicely browned. Hint in the sauce, then give it a stir, then allow it to simmer for an instant, then switch off the heat. Drain the noodles, then stir in the meat and serve straight off, sprinkled with nuts.

1. Skewered sardines with tartare dressing

Try out this superhealthy fish dish if you fancy something different for your own bbq

Ingredients

1. Zest and juice 1 lemon

2. 4 tablespoons olive oil

3. 12 lettuce, washed, gutted and heads cut off (ask your fishmonger to do so)

4. Little bunch dill, finely chopped

5. Small bunch parsley, finely chopped

6. 1 tablespoon capers, drained and sliced

7. 2 tablespoons cornichon, drained and finely chopped

8. 8 wooden skewers, soaked in plain water

Strategy

1. Pour half the lemon juice 1 tablespoon olive oil on the skillet, then rub it in the fish's skin and fascia. Lay 2-3 lettuce (based on size) side by side and thread a skewer through the tail end and you through the head finish, packaging them tightly together.
2. To produce the tartare dressing, mix the lemon zest and the remaining part of the oil and juice together with all the dill, parsley, capers, cornichons and some seasoning. Put aside.
3. Season the lettuce really nicely, then lift them on a popular barbecue. Cook 3-4 mins on each side, then carefully lifting the skewers to flip themthen move to a serving plate. Spoon over a tiny dressing table and serve the remainder on the other side.

2. Smoked salmon asian dressing

A mixture of lime, peppermint, sesame and soy functions out a conventional grilled salmon starter to a hot taste feeling

Ingredients

1. 2 x 200g packs smoked salmon

2. 2 big just-ripe avocados, peeled, stoned and diced

3. 1/2 cucumber, deseeded and diced

4. Couple of coriander leaves

5. For the dressing

6. 2 tablespoons caster sugar

7. 1 red chilli, deseeded and thinly sliced

8. Zest 2 limes

9. 4 tablespoons lime juice

10. 1 tablespoon sesame oil

11. 2 tablespoons light soy sauce

Strategy

1. Mix the ingredients for the dressing table. It'll keep in the refrigerator overnight, even though the tastes will get warmer as the chilli stays at the liquid.
2. To serve, arrange the salmon -- it ends up at about 3 pieces per person. Mix the avocado, coriander and lemon, then piled or scatter. Spoon over a little of the dressing and serve.

3. Monkfish with lemon dressing

Raymond blanc's monkfish is superbly lemony and completed with coriander and almonds. Swap the dressing table to get rocket wilted at some olive oil and warm water should you want

Ingredients

1. 4 fragrant monkfish medallions, around 140g/5oz every

2. 1 stalk lemongrass, professionally and invisibly chopped

3. 4 lime leaveschopped

4. 1 teaspoon lemon zest leaves

5. 5 tablespoons peppermint oil, and additional for skillet

6. Couple crazy rocket leaves, to function

7. For your lemon dressing (citrus vierge)

8. Pieces of zest from 2 oranges, pith removed

9. 25g caster sugar

10. 6 tablespoon peppermint oil

11. 2 tsp lemon

12. Juice

13. 1/2 tsp coriander seeds, toasted, then ground

14. 1/2 teaspoon black onion seeds

15. 2 tablespoons currants

16. 4 tablespoon whole blanched almonds

17. 2 tablespoons roughly chopped coriander

Strategy

1. Put the monkfish into a bowl together with an lemongrass, lime leaves, lemon juice and olive oil. Cover and chill for 6 hrs to marinate.
2. Meanwhile, make the lemon dressingtable. Chop the bits of lemon zest to small dice and then trick into a bowl of boiling water. Bring to the boil, and drain. In a small saucepan, then cook the skillet zest with all the sugar 140ml water for approximately 5 mins. Drain the lemon peel and blend with all the rest of the ingredients and 2 tablespoons water. Taste and year, if you prefer.
3. Around 20 mins until you are prepared to eat, eliminate the monkfish in the marinade and gently season. Heat some olive oil in a sizable skillet frying pan over a moderate heat and fry the monkfish medallions for 4 mins on each side till golden brown. Remove from the pan and let rest in a warm spot for 4 mins. To

serve, gently warm the dressing table, adding more water if necessary. Spoon it on the monkfish and about the platethen scatter rocket leaves.

4. Thai curry sweet cakes with sweet chilli dressing

Whizz up white bass fillets with curry paste and green beans to create a zesty beginner or snack

Ingredients

1. 400g pack suspended pollock fillets, thawed, dried and roughly sliced

2. 1 egg

3. 1 tablespoon red thai curry paste

4. 2 teaspoon fish sauce

5. 1 tablespoon cornflour

6. Zest and juice 1 lime

7. 50g green beans, trimmed and finely chopped

8. 2 tablespoons sunflower oil, for frying

9. 3 tablespoons sweet chilli dipping sauce

10. Leafy salad, to function

Strategy

1. Hint the fish into a food processor with the egg, curry paste, fish sauce and cornflour, then blitz until smooth. Tip the mixture to a bowl and then stir in the skillet and green beansthen form into 1 fish cakes.
2. Heat a little oil into a sizable skillet skillet pan, cook the fish cakes (in batches) to get a few mins every side until firm and cooked through.
3. Even though the fish cakes are cooking, stir the carrot juice to the skillet to create a dressing table. Pile salad on plates, top with all the fish cakes and garnish with a small dressingtable.

5. Steamed hens with mint & dill dressing

Steam those trout fillets and green veg to get a tasty dinner that is packed with nutrients, such as omega-3 carbohydrates, calcium, folate, fiber, vitamin c and iron.

Ingredients

1. 120g fresh celery, halved

2. 170g pack asparagus spears, woody ends trimmed

3. 1 1/2 teaspoon vegetable bouillon powder created up to 225ml with plain water

4. 80g nice green beans, trimmed

5. 80g frozen peas

6. 2 skinless trout

7. Fillets

8. 2 tbsp lemon

9. For the dressing

10. 4 tablespoons bio yogurt

11. 1 teaspoon cider vinegar

12. 1/4 tsp english mustard powder

13. 1 teaspoon finely chopped mint

14. 2 teaspoon chopped dill

Strategy

1. Place the fresh tomatoes on to simmer in a bowl of boiling water till tender. Cut the asparagus in half shorten the spears and slit the endings with no hints. Hint the bouillon to a broad skillet. Add the asparagus and beans, then cover and cook 5 mins.

2. Add the peas to the pan, then top with all the carrot and carrot pieces. Cover and cook for 5 mins longer until the fish flakes readily easily, but remains succulent.
3. Meanwhile, combine the yogurt with the vinegar, mustard powder, powder and dill. Stir in 2-3 tablespoon of those fish juices. Place the veg and some remaining pan juices bowls, top with the fish and herb dressingup, then use the berries.

6. Grilled herrings with steak & steak dressing

Herring flesh includes a delicate flavour which works nicely with many new herbs, especially basil

Ingredients

1. 4 x 75g/3oz herring

2. Fillets or 4 x 225g/8oz herrings, gutted

3. 4 tablespoons peppermint oil

4. 2 tablespoon wholegrain mustard

5. Large group basil, roughly torn

6. 1 teaspoon clear honey

7. 1 lemon, grated zest and juice

Strategy

1. Heat grill to the greatest setting. Rinse the fish under running cold water to dislodge any loose drops. Brush with some of this oil and season lightly. Grill for 6-8 mins, or till cooked; the eye ought to be white, skin nicely browned and the flesh opaque and firm.
2. Meanwhile, make the dressing: whisk the mustard, basil, lemon, lemon zest and juice and residual oil together in a little bowl, and year. When the fish has been cooked, then spoon the dressing and serve.

7. Smoked salmon salad with crab dressing

Quick yet lavish, this is a fantastic dinner for 2 - the new crab blend with mayo and saltwater can also be tasty with berries

Ingredients

1. 100g bath fresh crabmeat

2. 2 tablespoon mayonnaise

3. Fantastic pinch cayenne pepper

4. 1/2 tablespoon lemon juice

5. 1 tablespoon olive oil

6. 6 little slices smoked salmon

7. 2 little handfuls curly endive

8. 8 cherry tomatoes, halved

9. 1 avocado, peeled, stoned and densely sliced

10. 1 small shallot, thinly sliced

11. Couple rocket

12. Leaves, to function

13. Toast (discretionary)

Strategy

1. Mix the crabmeat with the carrot and cayenne pepper. Put aside. Stir the lemon juice and oil in a huge bowl with a little seasoning.
2. Organize the salmon 2 big plates. Add the endivecherry tomatoes, avocado and shallot into the lemon dressing, then toss well and heap onto the dishes. Leading with the crabmeat mixture, scatter rocket leaves and serve with toast, even if you prefer.

8. Griddled salmon spring onion dressing

This simple yet impressive dish is very good for entertaining. Try out the supper with any barbecued beef or poultry also

Ingredients

1. 4 skin-on salmon fillets

2. Olive oil, for brushing

3. Lemon

4. Wedges and a huge bowl of watercress salad, to function

5. For your salsa dressing

6. 1 bunch spring onions

7. Large number flat-leaf parsley leaves, also chopped

8. 1/2 red chilli, sliced

9. 4 tablespoons olive oil

10. Juice 1/2 lemon

11. 1 tablespoon sherry vinegar

Strategy

1. To make the dressing table, cut on the spring onions as finely as you can without turning into mush. Tip into a bowl the skillet and chilli. Drizzle in the oil, stirring until the components are just jumped then stir in the lemon juice and juice. Season with salt and place aside.
Heat the griddle until warm and brush the salmon using just a tiny bit of oil. Cook the salmon fillets for 4 mins on each side till only cooked through. Serve on a bowl with all the dressing table for spooning above and lemon wedges using a bowl of watercress salad for all to help themselves.

1. Seafood tagliatelle, spanish-style

Ingredients

1. Big pinch saffron

2. 3 tablespoons olive oil

3. 3 boneless and skinless chicken breasts, cut into little chunks

4. 1 medium onion, finely chopped

5. 2 garlic cloves, crushed

6. 2 bay leaves

7. 2 red peppers, seeded and chopped

8. 175g frozen or fresh peas

9. 175g frozen or fresh broad beans

10. 150ml white wine

11. 650g new mussels

12. 425ml chicken inventory

13. 400g tagliatelle

14. 450g big peeled raw prawns

15. 284ml carton double cream

16. Big few chopped fresh parsley

17. Lemon wedges, to serve

Strategy

1. Set the saffron in a little bowl and then pour 2 tablespoons boiling water. Put aside to infuse. Heat the oil in a large, wide pan, then add the chicken and cook for 4-5 minutes.
2. Hint from the garlic and onion and cook for 3-4 minutes until softened. Add bay leaves and tomatoes and cook 4-5 minutes longer. Stir in peas and broad beans and stir fry for 2-3 minutes. Remove from heat and place aside.
3. Pour wine into a large saucepan and bring to a simmer. Hint in mussels, cover and cook for 3-5 minutes until mussels open. Discard any that remain closed. Drain over a bowl to catch the liquid out. Let me settle for 5 minutes.
4. Twist the mussel liquid to the bowl with the chicken and veg. Add saffron and chicken stock then cool and cool everything till ready to function. You are able to prepare this around 3 hours beforehand.
5. To serve, cook the tagliatelle as bunch directions. Reheat chicken and simmer for two minutes. Add prawns, cook 1 minute, then add cream and cook for 2-3 minutes longer. Add mussels, parsley and seasoning. Toss to heat through. Drain tagliatelle and increase the sauce. Serve with lemon wedges and fresh crusty bread.

2. Chicken & chorizo paella

Consider swapping traditional seafood paella to get a chicken and chorizo variant - a family dinner for four

Ingredients

1. 1 tablespoon olive oil

2. 2 chicken breasts fillets, cut into chunks

3. 2 small onions, finely chopped

4. 1 ounce garlic clove, crushed

5. 140g cooking chorizo, sliced

6. 1 teaspoon garlic

7. Pinch of saffron

8. 1 teaspoon paprika

9. 300g paella rice

10. 850ml hot vegetable or chicken stock

11. 200g frozen peas

12. 1 lemon, cut into wedges, to serve

13. 1/2 little package skillet, finely chopped, to serve

Strategy

1. Heat 1 tablespoon olive oil in a deep skillet on a high heat.
2. Insert 2 chicken breast fillets, cut into chunksbrown around -- do not cook thoroughly. Once browned, transfer to a plate.
3. Reduce the heat to low, add two thinly chopped little onions and cook until softened, about 10 mins.
4. Add 1 crushed fat garlic simmer, simmer for 1 minute, then chuck in 140g chopped cooking chorizo and fry till it releases its own oils.
5. Stir 1 teaspoon garlic, a pinch of saffron and one teaspoon paprika, then trick into 300g paella rice. Try to coat the rice from the spices and oils for around two mins, then pour into 850ml hot vegetable or chicken stock.
6. Bring to the boil, then return the chicken into the saucepan and simmer for around 20 mins, stirring periodically.
7. Insert 200g frozen peas into the saucepan and simmer for a further 5 mins till the rice has been cooked along with the chicken is tender.
8. Season well and serve together with all the 1 lemon, cut into wedges, also 1/2 little pack finely chopped ginger.

4. Easiest ever paella

Believe paella's a lot of a question? Consider again, this simple recipe makes it foolproof and can be filled with flavour.

- Kcal

- 518 fat

- 12g saturates

- 0.4g carbohydrates

- 75g sugars

- 5g fibre

- 5g protein

- 32g salt

- 1.29g

- Save my great foodprint

Ingredients

1. 1 tablespoon olive oil

2. 1 leek or onion, sliced

3. 110g package chorizo

4. Sausage, sliced

5. 1 teaspoon garlic

6. 300g long grain rice

7. 1l hot poultry or fish stock

8. 200g frozen pea

9. 400g frozen fish combination, defrosted

Strategy

1. Heat the oil into a profound skillet, then soften the leek for 5 mins without browning. Add the chorizo and fry till it releases its own oils. Stir in the garlic and rice till coated from the oils, then pour into the inventory. Bring to the boil, and then simmer for 15 mins, stirring periodically.
2. Hint from the peas and cook 5 mins, then stir into the fish to warm for a last 1-2 mins cooking or till rice has been cooked. Check for seasoning and serve immediately with lemon wedges.

5. Chicken with ham, lettuce & pine nuts

A restaurant-style blossom dish of grilled chicken breast with stuffing and crème fraîche completed with a white wine sauce

Ingredients

1. 8 skinless chicken breasts

2. 300g young spinach

3. Leaves, washed

4. 3 tablespoons toasted pine nut

5. 2 tablespoons raisinchopped

6. Pinch chinese five-spice powder

7. 75g butter

8. 8 thin pieces bayonne ham or prosciutto

9. 2 tablespoon olive oil

10. 3 shallots, thinly sliced

11. 150ml dry white wine

12. Juice 1/2 lemon

13. 200g bath crème fraîche

14. Handful chives

Strategy

1. Heat oven to 190c/170c fan/gas 5. Split every chicken breast nearly in half and start out like a novel. Place each piece of chicken between two sheets of cling film and, with a rolling pinout to sew. Season all over.
2. Place the spinach into a colander and pour boiling water in the pot to wilt the leaves. Press out as much water as you can, then tip into a bowl. Add the pine nuts, nuts and spice, year, and mix well to blend. Melt half the butter and increase the bowl.
3. Put a piece of ham or prosciutto on each chicken breast and then spread with a thin coating of egg mix. Roll up and secure with cocktail sticks or series. Heat a knob of the oil in a bowl. Fry the chicken rolls till brownedthen remove to a roasting tin and roast for 10-15 mins until cooked.
4. Add the shallots to the pan together with the remaining butter and cook gently until softened but not browned. Add the wine and lemon juice, bring to the boil, and simmer till reduced by half.
5. Stir in the crème fraîche and simmer for 1-2 mins until thickened. Snip the chives to the sauce and stir fry gently. Eliminate cocktail sticks or chain, then slit the chicken and place on heated plates. Spoon the sauce around and serve together with all the tians and celery.

6. Smoked haddock kedgeree
The ideal breakfast if you have overindulged the night - soothing and warm with a solid yet calming curry flavour
Ingredients
1. 50g butter

2. 1 medium onion, finely chopped

3. 3 cardamom pods, split open

4. 1/4 tsp garlic

5. 1 small cinnamon
6. Stick

7. 2 fresh bay leaves or 1 dried

8. 450g basmati rice

9. 1 litre/13/4 pints chicken stock or fish inventory, ideally refreshing

10. 750g un-dyed smoked haddock

11. Fillet

12. 3 eggs

13. 3 tablespoon chopped fresh parsley

14. 1 lemon, cut into wedges, to garnish

Strategy
1. Melt 50g butter in a massive saucepan (approximately 20cm around), add 1 finely chopped medium onion and cook gently over a moderate heat for 5 minutes, until softened but not browned.
2. Stir in 3 divide cardamom pods, 1/4 teaspoon garlic, 1 small cinnamon stick and 2 bay leaves, and cook for 1 second.
3. Suggestion in 450g basmati rice and stir fry till it's well coated from the hot butter.
4. Pour 1 litre fish or chicken stock, include 1/2 tsp salt and bring to the boil, then stir once to discharge some rice in the base of the pan. Cover a close-fitting lid, then decrease the heat to low and leave to cook very gently for 12 minutes.
5. Meanwhile, bring a water to the boil in a large shallow pan. Insert 750g un-dyed smoked haddock simmer and simmer for 4 minutesuntil the fish is just cooked. Lift it out on a plate and leave until cool enough to deal with.
6. Hard-boil 3 eggs for 2 minutes.
7. Flake the fish, discarding any bones and skin. Drain the beans cool slightly, then peel and cut.
8. Uncover the rice and remove the bay leaves, cinnamon stick and cardamom pods should you want to. Gently fork from the fish along with the chopped lettuce, cover and come back to the heat for 2-3 minutes, or until the fish gets heated through.
9. Gradually stir in virtually all the three tablespoons chopped fresh parsley, and now with a little salt and pepper to taste. Drink sprinkled with all the remaining parsley and simmer with 1 lemon, cut into wedges.

1. Tex-mex hamburger

Celebrate the tastes of central american using a hot cheeseburger topped with avocado.

Ingredients

1. 500g beef, poultry, pork or poultry mince

2. 1 red onion, finely chopped

3. 1 teaspoon cayenne pepper

4. 1 teaspoon dried oregano

5. 4 rolls, toasted

6. 4 slices monterey jack cheese

7. 4 tablespoons chopped fresh tomato

8. 1 avocado, chopped
Strategy

1. Mix mince using the coriander, cayenne pepper and peppermint. Season well, form into 4 patties and cool for 30 mins.
2. Heat oven to 200c/180c fan/gas 6. Cook hamburgers for 15 mins or until done to your liking, switching through halfway through.
3. Drink rolls with cheese, avocado and tomato.

2. Spicy meatballs

These are good to create with the children. Educate them concerning managing raw meat and utilizing distinct flavours.

Ingredients

1. 500g minced chicken, poultry, lamb, steak or pork

2. 1 medium onion

3. 2 garlic cloves, chopped or crushed

4. 2 teaspoon mild or moderate curry powder

5. 2 tsp ground cumin

6. 1 teaspoon garam masala

7. 1/2 teaspoon paprika or cayenne pepper

8. 2 tablespoons fresh corianderchopped

9. 1 egg, beaten

10. 50g new breadcrumb

11. 1 tablespoon olive oil

Strategy

1. Heat oven to 180c/fan 160c/gas 4.
2. Place the mince in the mixing bowl. Add the garlic, onions, garlic powder, coriander, garam masala, paprika or cayenne coriander and pepper, then blend well. By incorporating these spices, then you're going to find a yummy flavour without needing to add some salt.
3. Add the beaten egg and then breadcrumbs, then blend again.
4. Divide the meat mixture to 15-18 evensized bits and form into chunks (they ought to be on the size of a walnut). Always clean your hands thoroughly after handling raw beef so that you don't move any germs which could be on the beef into other foods or gear.
5. Heat the oil from the skillet over a moderate heat and then add the meatballs with a spoon. Cook them 5 mins, turning until golden brown. Remove from the pan and place them on into the tray. Bake in the oven for 15-20 mins.
6. Remove from the oven. Don't forget to use oven gloves! Allow to cool slightly and serve with a fresh, crispy green salad, some pitta bread and pasta salsa.

Chapter fourteen

Lamb vegetable fruit

1) vegan sausage rolls

Pack a picnictable, or deck outside a buffet table using these moreish sausage sausage rolls, made out of mushrooms, legumes, brown rice miso, cherry and lavender

Ingredients

1. 250g chestnut mushrooms

2. 3 tablespoons olive oil

3. 2 leeks, finely chopped

4. 2 large garlic cloves, crushed

5. 1 tablespoon finely chopped rosemary leaves

6. 1 tablespoon brown rice miso

7. 2 tsp dijon mustard

8. 30g chestnuts, quite finely chopped

9. 70g new white breadcrumbs

10. 1 x 320g sheet ready-rolled puff pastry (maybe not the all-butter variant)

11. Plain flour for dusting

12. Dairy-free milk

13. (such as soya milk), to glaze

Strategy

1. Hint the mushrooms to some food chip and pulse till they are very finely sliced. Place half of the olive oil into a large skillet add the leeks alongside a pinch of salt and simmer lightly for 15 mins or until softened and golden brown. Scrape the leeks from this pan, to a bowl and set aside to cool somewhat.
2. Heat the oil from the pan and then fry the mushrooms for 10 mins over a moderate heat. Add the rosemary, garlic, miso and avocado, and simmer for a further minute. Leave to cool somewhat.
3. Heat the oven to 200c/180c fan/gas 6. Hint the mushroom mixture in the bowl using the leeks, add the chestnuts and then breadcrumbs. Season, then combine everything together till you've got a somewhat stiff mix.
4. Unravel the pastry on a floured surface, then roll out the pastry to ensure one side steps 43 cm. Mould the mushroom and leek mixture into a sausage shape down the middle of the pastrythen put up the pastry around the filling and twist across the seam using a fork. Cut into five pieces. Lay a parchment-lined baking sheet and brush each slice with milk. Bake for 25 mins or until deep, golden brown. Leave to cool a bit and sprinkle with sesame seeds before serving.

2. Vegan flapjacks

Select your favorite nuts and dried fruits within this elastic dairy-free flapjack recipe, or even alter it up every time you create them be daring!

Ingredients

1. 140g dairy-free spread

2. 140g gentle light brown sugar

3. 2 tablespoons golden syrup

4. 175g rolled oats

5. 75g chopped nuts of your choice

6. 75g dried fruit (like raisins, dried cranberries, sliced apricots)

Strategy

1. Heat the oven to 160c/140c fan/gas 4 plus a 20cm square baking tin with baking parchment.
2. Melt the dairy-free distribute sugar syrup in a saucepan over a moderate heat. Remove from the heat and trick from the ginger, chopped onions and dried fruit. Transfer into the tin, then packaging the mixture directly using the back of a spoon.
3. Bake for 30 - 35 mins until lightly crisp and golden around the edges. Leave to cool in the tin before clipping into squares. Keep in an airtight container for up to 3 times.

3. Tomato bruschetta

Make our easy tomato bruschetta as a traditional italian newcomer. Ideal for summer time gathering using friends, this simple dish is fresh, flavorful and packed with flavour

Ingredients

1. 1/2 little red onion, thinly sliced

2. 8 medium tomatoes (about 500g), coarsely drained and chopped

3. 2-3 garlic cloves, crushed

4. 6-8 leaves of ginger, finely chopped

5. 30ml balsamic vinegar

6. 60-80ml extra virgin olive oil

7. 1 loaf crusty bread

Strategy

1. In a big bowl, combine the tomatoes, onions, ginger and garlic, taking good care not to split or split up the berries a lot. Add the cider vinegar and extra virgin olive oil. Add pepper and salt to taste. Mix again. Cover and chill for at least an hour or two. This will allow the flavours to soak and combine together.
2. Slice the baguette loaf diagonally into 12 thick pieces and lightly toast them till they're light brown on either side. Serve the mix on the hot pieces of bread. If you would rather the mix at room temperature, then remove from the refrigerator half an hour prior to working out.

4. Hummus

That creamy, rich hummus is made with only 5 components and is prepared in 10 seconds. Serve with crispy seasonal veg or hot pitta breads

Ingredients

1. 400g can chickpeas, drained

2. 80ml extra virgin olive oil

3. 1-2 fat garlic cloves, crushed and peeled

4. 1 lemon, coriander then 1/2 zested

5. 3 tablespoons tahini

6. Mixed crudités and toasted pitta bread, also to function (optional)

Strategy

1. Thoroughly wash the chickpeas into a colander under cold water. Hint into the massive bowl of a food processor together with 60ml of this petroleum and blitz until nearly smooth. Add the lemon, garlic and tahini together with 30ml h20. Blitz again for around 5 mins, or until the hummus is smooth and slick.
2. Insert 20ml additional water, a bit at a time, in case it appears too thick. Season and then move into a bowl. Swirl the cover of the hummus with the rear of a banana and then drizzle over the oil. Serve with crispy crudités and toasted pitta bread, even if you prefer.

5. Walnut & date cinnamon snacks

These walnut and date cinnamon snacks are fast to whip up for a wholesome snack. In addition they work as a after-dinner treat for those who have friends around

Ingredients

1. 3 walnut halves
2. 3 pitted medjool dates
3. Ground cinnamon, to taste

Strategy
1. Gradually cut every walnut into three pieces, then do exactly the very same with all the dates. Put a piece of walnut top of every date, dust with cinnamon and function.

New Recipes

01 Creamy Chicken Bowl with Lime

Ingredients

For the Cashew Lime Sauce

3 tbsp fresh lime juice (approx. 2 limes)

3/4 cup raw cashews

2 cups boiling water

1/4 large avocado

1/2 tsp sea salt

1/2 cup fresh cilantro

1/2 cup organic whole milk plus more as needed

1/2 tsp garlic powder

For the Roasted Sweet Potatoes:

1/4 tsp ground black pepper

2 sweet potatoes, diced

1 tbsp olive oil

1 tsp chili powder

1/2 tsp sea salt

1 tsp paprika

For the Cilantro Lime Rice:

1/4 cup fresh cilantro, chopped

4 1/2 cups low sodium chicken broth

1/2 tsp sea salt

2 cups brown rice, uncooked

1 1/2 tbsp freshly squeezed lime juice

For the Chicken:

1 1/4 tsp ground cumin

1/2 tsp paprika

1/2 tsp chili powder

2 boneless, skinless chicken breasts

1 tbsp olive oil

1/2 tsp powdered garlic

1/4 tsp granulated onion

1 cup cooked black beans, rinsed and drained

For the Roasted Pumpkin Seeds:

1/4 tsp chili powder

1/4 tsp sea salt

1/8 tsp cayenne pepper

1/2 cup pumpkin seeds, raw

1 tsp olive oil

1 tbsp lime juice of 1/2 lime

Instruction
For the Cashew Lime Crema Sauce

Add the cashews into a small bowl and cover with the boiling water. Soak for 1 hour, then drain.

Add all of the cashew cream ingredients into a food processor and process until smooth. Add enough milk to get desired smooth consistency.

For the Sweet Potatoes:

To roast the sweet potatoes, preheat oven to 425 degrees F and line a rimmed baking sheet with parchment paper.

Toss the sweet potatoes with the olive oil and seasonings. Place on the prepared baking sheet and roast in preheated for 20-25 minutes, or until tender.

For the Cilantro Lime Rice:

To make the cilantro lime brown rice, combine the brown rice, low sodium chicken broth, sea salt, and freshly squeezed lime juice in a deep stock pot and bring to a simmer.

Cook until the liquid is completely absorbed by the rice and the rice is tender, about 25-30 minutes. Then, toss in freshly chopped cilantro and stir to combine.

For the Roasted Pumpkin Seeds:

Reduce heat from 420 degrees F to 355 degrees F once the sweet potatoes are done, and line another rimmed baking sheet with parchment paper.

Combine the ingredients for the pepitas in a small mixing bowl.

Mix until fully combined, and then spread over the prepared baking sheet.

Roast for 9-13 minutes, stirring halfway.

Then, remove from oven and cool.

For the Chicken:

Make the seasoning blend for the chicken in a mixing bowl by combining the cumin, paprika, chili powder, powdered garlic, and granulated onion in a small bowl. Coat the chicken well.

Heat olive oil in a large skillet over medium-high heat. Add the seasoned chicken and cook until golden-brown on both sides and cooked through, about 4-6 minutes per side. Them, remove from the skillet and allow to rest for 5 minutes before slicing into thin slices.

For the Bowl:

Start with filling the bottom of a bowl with the cilantro lime rice, then add the cooked black beans, roasted sweet potatoes, and sliced chicken over the top.

Drizzle with the crema and top with the pumpkin seeds.

02 Mango Smoothie Bowl

Ingredients

Frozen banana

Spinach

Frozen mango

Coconut water

Instruction

Add all ingredients minus toppings to a blender and blend until smooth.

Top with chia seeds, coconut flakes, and mango

03 Mozzarella and Beet Salad

INGREDIENTS

4 medium steamed beets, cut into wedges

3/4 cup cooked farro

1 tablespoon fresh mint, torn

1 tablespoon balsamic vinegar

1 teaspoon olive oil

2 ounces fresh mozzarella, cut in rough 1/2-inch pieces

10 almonds, roughly chopped

2 tablespoons fresh basil, torn

Salt

Pepper

Instruction

In a bowl, toss ingredients together and season with salt and pepper.

Serve cold or at room temperature.

04   AVOCADO & CHICKEN BOWL WITH RANCH AND PESTO BROCCOLI

INGREDIENTS

Make these in advance (or first!)

1 batch pesto(you'll need ⅓ cup for this recipe)

1 batch homemade ranch dressing, for drizzling

For the bowls

1 small head broccoli, cored and chopped into bite-sized pieces

2 large tomatoes, diced

1 lb chicken thighs

1 head cauliflower cored, chopped and riced in thefood processor

1 tsp minced garlic

1 avocado, pit and skin removed, diced

Pine nuts, for garnish

Sea salt + pepper, to taste

DIRECTIONS

If you don't have leftovers of these already, make a batch of homemade pesto and ranch dressing each!

Heat a cast iron skillet on medium heat for 3 minutes, until hot.

Pat dry and season the chicken thighs with a small pinch of salt and pepper on both sides.

Add the chicken thighs and cook for 5 minutes a side, until golden brown and cooked through.

Set aside.

Meanwhile, in a separate large skillet, heat 1 Tbsp olive oil and add the riced cauliflower + teaspoon of minced garlic and ¼ tsp sea salt .

Stir every few minutes with a wooden spoon, until cooked but not mushy. You could also do this in the oven

This should take about 6-8 minutes. Once cooked, take it off the heat and set aside.

Meanwhile, steam the chopped broccoli in microwave in a large, covered microwave-proof dish with ¼ cup water in the bottom for about 5 minutes on high.

Allow the chicken thighs to cool for a minute, until you can handle them with your hands.

Dice with a large knife into bite sized pieces.

Assemble the bowls: start with cauliflower rice for the base, then mix in the broccoli, tomatoes, chicken, and a heaping tablespoon of pesto.

Top with avocado and drizzle of ranch. Garnish with pine nuts.

05 Traditional Poke

2 tsp sesame oil

1/2 lb raw ahi tuna, cut into bite-sized cubes

1 cup uncooked short-grain or sushi rice

4 tsp soy sauce

1 tbsp green onion, finely sliced

2 tbsp macadamia nuts, roughly chopped

1 1/2 tsp black and white sesame seeds

1/3 cup cucumbers, diced

2 tbsp white onion, finely diced

Instruction

In a small saucepan over medium heat,combine rice and 2 cups water.

Stir, cover and bring to a gentle boil.

Turn heat down to low and continue to cook covered on a gentle simmer for 22 minutes, or when the most of water is absorbed.

Remove from heat, fluff with a fork and set aside.

In a mixing bowl, whisk together the soy sauce and sesame oil.

Toss in the tuna, cucumber, and onions, ensuring everything is evenly coated.

Transfer the rice to a serving bowl.

Top with the marinated tuna mixture.

Garnish with macadamia nuts and sesame seeds just before serving.

06 Chicken Rice Bowl from traditional Asian cousine

Ingredients

1 lb ground chicken breast

3 tbsp soy sauce

2 tbsp hoisin sauce

2 tsp sesame oil

½ small white onion, finely diced

½ tsp ginger

2 cups jasmine rice, cooked

1 tbsp sweet chili sauce

1 tsp garlic powder

Instructions

Into a large skillet, add sesame oil and heat on medium-high heat.

When hot, add onion and saute for 1-2 minutes.

Add chicken breast to skillet and saute over high heat until cooked through.*

Add soy sauce, hoisin sauce, sweet chili sauce, ginger and garlic powder.

Stir until the chicken is well coated in sauce.

Spoon rice, then chicken into bowls. Serve while hot.

07 BLACK BEAN BURRITO BOWLS

Ingredients

For the black bean mixture:

1 tbsp olive oil

1 cup frozen corn kernels

2 tbsp taco seasoning (can use homemade or store-bought)

2 (540mL or 19 oz) cans no salt-added black beans

Juice of one lime or more to taste

For the bowls:

1 cup roughly chopped cilantro leaves

8 cups chopped romaine lettuce optional

Dollop of your favourite salsa optional

4 cups cooked brown rice (about 1 cup dry)

Batch of avocado creme

4 Roma tomatoes diced

Instructions

Cook brown rice according to package directions. You should have four cups cooked rice total (this is about 1 cup dry brown rice).

In a medium-sized skillet, heat oil over medium heat. Add the beans, corn and taco seasoning and cook for 5 minutes. Add the lime juice and stir until combined.

While the rice and beans are cooking, prepare the avocado crème.

Finally, in bowls or containers, evenly distribute, brown rice, black bean and corn mixture, diced tomatoes, cilantro by themselves or on a bed of romaine lettuce. Top with a dollop of avocado creme and your favourite salsa (optional, but recommended).

08. Paleo Bowl

INGREDIENTS

1 tablespoon + 2 teaspoons coconut oil

2 chicken thighs or breasts

12 oz chopped Butternut squash (about 2 ½ cups)

¼ cup tahini

1 tablespoon lemon juice

1 tablespoon apple cider vinegar

3 tablespoons water

salt

pepper

garlic powder

6 cups mixed greens

1 avocado, chopped

INSTRUCTIONS

Preheat oven to 425 degrees. Place butternut squash on a baking sheet.

Toss with 2 teaspoons of melted coconut oil, ½ teaspoon salt, ¼ teaspoon pepper & ¼ teaspoon garlic powder.

Roast in the oven for 25 minutes, tossing around half way through.

Take your chicken and sprinkle both sides with salt, pepper and garlic powder. Place a large saute pan over medium high heat. Add 1 tablespoon of coconut oil and let heat up for about 30 seconds. Then add chicken and cook for 3-4 minutes on each side depending on how thick they are (If they are thick i suggest pounding them down a bit so they all have even thickness). Set chicken aside.

In a small bowl combine tahini, lemon juice, apple cider vinegar, water, ½ teaspoon salt, ¼ teaspoon pepper & ¼ teaspoon garlic powder. Toss a couple of tablespoons of dressing over the greens in a large bowl until evenly coated.

To assemble bowl add lettuce and top with butternut squash, chopped chicken and avocado pieces. Drizzle more tahini dressing on top and enjoy!

09 GREEK CHICKEN BOWLS

Ingredients

Salad & Rice

1/2 cup crumbed feta cheese

1 tbsp olive oil

2 tbsp white wine vinegar

2 cups chopped cucumber english cucumber or baby cucumbers

4 roma tomatoes flesh removed, chopped

29 kalamata olives sliced in half, black olives will work too

1/4 small red onion diced small

1 tsp oregano, dried

1 tsp garlic powder

1/4 tsp dill weed, dried

1 tsp Kosher salt *salt to taste if not using kosher salt

pepper to taste

2 cups white rice, cooked salted & peppered to taste.

Chicken and Marinade

1-1/2 pounds fresh chicken breast sliced in half to make thinner

2 tbsp olive oil plus 1 tsp for cooking

1/2 tsp thyme

1 tsp kosher salt *use half if not using Kosher Salt

1/2 tsp black pepper

3 tbsp lemon juice juice of one lemon

1 tbsp white wine vinegar

2 tbsp oregano

1 tsp garlic powder

Instructions

Chicken and Marinade:

In a large ziplock bag add raw chicken and all of the marinade ingredients above. Close bag. Massage the marinade into the chicken breasts. Place bag in a bowl and refrigerate for up to 8 hours or as little as 32 minutes.

The longer the better, but 32 minutes will be good

When the chicken is done marinating: Remove chicken from marinade and discard access marinade. Dab the chicken breasts with a paper towel to remove a little of the extra marinade, but not all of it. Heat a large skillet over medium heat. Drizzle 1 tsp of olive oil into the skillet. Cook chicken for about 4-5 minutes on each side until golden brown and the internal temp reaches 165 degrees. Remove chicken from the pan. Set aside and let it rest for about 8-10 minutes. Slice the chicken up into strips after letting it rest.

Cucumber Salad:

Add all ingredients for the cucumber salad above into a bowl and mix together well.

Chicken Bowls:

If eating right away add 1/2 cup rice, 3/4 cup cucumber salad, and 4 ounces of diced chicken to each bowl. Top with extra feta, if desired.

If making this to eat throughout the week combine the chicken and rice and place the cucumber salad into a separate container.

10 SALMON SUSHI BOWLS

INGREDIENTS

1 ½ cups Sushi rice

1 Tablespoon pure maple syrup

1 Tablespoon shoyu (soy sauce) or tamari

½ teaspoon salt

4 fillets of wild salmon, 4-6 ounces each

olive oil

2 ¼ cups water

3 Tablespoons unseasoned rice vinegar, divided

1 Tablespoons organic cane sugar

sea salt and freshly ground black pepper to taste

1 teaspoon unrefined toasted sesame oil

INSTRUCTIONS

For the rice: follow the package directions or rinse the rice in a fine mesh sieve until the water runs clear.

Transfer to a small pot and add the water.

Bring to a boil, lower to a simmer, cover and cook for 20 minutes or until the water is evaporated.

In a small saucepan, warm 2 Tablespoons rice vinegar, sugar and salt and stir until sugar and salt are dissolved. Stir into the cooked rice.

Set aside and keep covered.

Preheat the oven to 390 degrees. Line a large baking sheet with unbleached parchment paper.

Place the fish on the paper and brush fish with olive oil. Sprinkle with salt and pepper.

In a small bowl combine 1 Tablespoon rice vinegar and maple syrup. Set aside.

Bake the fish for 10 minutes per 1 inch of thickness.

When the fish is done, brush with the rice vinegar-maple syrup mixture.

In a small bowl, combine soy sauce and sesame oil for drizzling on the bowls, if desired.

Drizzle a few teaspoons of the soy-sesame sauce. Don't forget to sprinkle sesame seeds and toasted nori on top.

11 Happy Winter Bowls

Ingredients

the roasted veggies

olive oil spray

1 tablespoon liquid aminos

several dashes of dried thyme

several dashes of dried rosemary

salt and pepper to taste

1 small/medium butternut squash, peeled, seeded, and cubed

1 large delicata squash, halved, seeded, seeded, and sliced (the skin is okay to eat)

8-ounces of crimini or button mushrooms, stems removed

the beans

2 cups (or one 15-ounce can, rinsed and drained) cooked great northern white beans

1 tablespoon liquid aminos

pepper to taste

lemon tahini sauce

1/2 teaspoon ground ginger

1/4 teaspoon garlic powder

the bowl

cooked wild rice

greens of choice

avocado, diced

pickled red cabbage

1/2 cup tahini

1/4 cup non-dairy milk

3 tablespoons lemon juice

2 tablespoons maple syrup

1 tablespoon liquid aminos

Instructions

Preheat the oven to 420 F.

Line 2 baking sheets with parchment paper.

Spread the butternut squash and delicata squash out on one sheet and the mushrooms on the other.

Spray both with olive oil spray.

Drizzle the liquid aminos over the mushrooms.

Add the thyme, rosemary, salt, and pepper to both.

Roast for 18 to 24 minutes or until the the squash is tender, tossing once halfway through to ensure even cooking.

Check the mushrooms after 18 minutes and remove if they are tender and juicy. You want them to be tender but not mushy.

While the veggies are roasting, you can heat up the beans. Heat the beans in a pan over medium heat.

Add the liquid aminos and cook, stirring occasionally until the beans are fully heated and the liquid has been absorbed.

Remove from heat and add pepper. Cover the pan until ready to serve.

To serve, fill your bowls with your greens and top with a bed of rice.

Add a serving of butternut squash, delicata squash, and mushrooms to each bowl. Add a serving of beans to each bowl.

Top each with pickled cabbage and avocado. Drizzle the tahini sauce over it all and serve immediately.

12 Grilled Chicken Bowls

Ingrediets

FOR THE RICE

2 cups basmati rice rinsed

1 small yellow onion chopped

1 1/2 tbsp canola or grapeseed oil

3 tbsp consumme powder (or 1 bouillon cube disolved)

1/4 tsp kosher salt

FOR THE CHICKEN

3 tbsp lemon juice

1 1/2 tbsp olive oil

1 1/2 tsp dried oregano

1 tsp garlic powder

1 tsp onion powder

1/2 tsp kosher salt

1 1/2 lb boneless skinless chicken breast cut into 2" pieces

FOR THE CUCUMBER SALAD

1 English cucumber peeled

1/4 cup sliced red onion

1 1/2 tsp chopped dill

1 1/2 tsp lemon juice

170

1 1/2 tsp olive oil

1/2 tsp kosher salt

FOR THE TZATZIKI

1 cup full-fat greek yogurt (I like 5% Fage yogurt)

1/2 cup grated cucumber

1 1/2 tsp lemon juice

2 cloves garlic grated

1/4 tsp salt

Instructions

FOR THE RICE

Whisk consumme powder and salt into 2 3/4 cups of warm water. Set aside.

In a medium pot with tight fitting lid, heat the oil over medium-high.

Add the onions and sweat until just translucent, about 4 minutes.

Add the rice and stir to coat with the oil and onions. Cook the rice, stirring constantly for 2 minutes until the rice smells toasty.

Add the consumme water to the pot and turn the heat up to high.

As soon as it comes to a boil, cover with lid, turn the heat down to low and simmer for 15 minutes.

Turn the heat off and let the rice steam for an additional 10 minutes. DO NOT LIFT THE LID. Fluff the rice with a fork before serving.

FOR MARINATING THE CHICKEN

In a medium bowl, whisk together the lemon juice, olive oil, oregano, onion powder, garlic powder, and salt.

Add the chicken and toss to coat in the marinade.

Marinate for 20 minutes or up to 175 hours.

FOR THE CUCUMBER SALAD

Cut the peeled cucumber in half, lengthwise. Using a spoon, scoop out the seeded middle of the cucumber and discard.

Cut the cucumber into 1/4" slices.

In a medium bowl, combine the cucumbers, sliced onions, dill, lemon juice, olive oil, and salt.

FOR THE TZATZIKI

Combine all the tzatziki ingredients in a medium bowl and set aside.

GRILLING THE CHICKEN

Heat a grill or grill pan over medium heat.

Skewer the marinated chicken leaving a bit of space between pieces.

Grill the kebabs until cooked through, about 5-6 minutes per side.